GETHIN HUGHES is a member of the Department of Spanish and Portuguese at the University of Toronto.

Francisco de la Torre has long been praised as an outstanding poet in the mould of Garcilaso de la Vega and his simplicity of style and the soft, gentle, Arcadian environment of his poetry have been emphasized.

In this volume Professor Hughes attempts to define more accurately the position of Francisco de la Torre's verse in the evolution of Spanish poetry in the sixteenth century, revealing that Torre's vision of the pastoral world and his poetic language show him to be a transitional poet of considerable quality and substance and not merely an imitator of Garcilaso.

Hughes demonstrates that while some of Torre's poetry follows a general pastoral pattern, his descriptions are characterized by a sense of movement through a shifting of perspective and that even in poems with a traditional pastoral setting, the descriptions sometimes negate the pastoral qualities. The author also shows that Torre, rather than looking back towards Garcilaso and his contemporaries, is already anticipating – especially in his stylistic technique and in his view of nature – the attitude of the seventeenth century.

GETHIN HUGHES

The Poetry of
Francisco de la Torre

UNIVERSITY OF TORONTO PRESS
Toronto Buffalo London

University of Toronto Romance Series 43

© University of Toronto Press 1982
Toronto Buffalo London
Reprinted in paperback 2017

ISBN 978-0-8020-2427-5 (cloth)
ISBN 978-1-4875-9185-4 (paper)

Canadian Cataloguing in Publication Data

Hughes, John Gethin, 1939-
The poetry of Francisco de la Torre

Bibliography: p.
Includes index.
ISBN 978-0-8020-2427-5 (bound)   ISBN 978-1-4875-9185-4 (pbk.)

1. Torre, Francisco de la, 1534?-1594 – Criticism
and interpretation. I. Title.

PQ6437.T74Z72   861'.3   C82-094560-9

This book has been published with the help of a grant from the
Canadian Federation for the Humanities, using funds provided by the
Social Sciences and Humanities Research Council of Canada,
and a grant from the Publications Fund of the
University of Toronto Press.

Contents

THE POETRY OF FRANCISCO DE LA TORRE

Introduction

On 17 September 1629, Lorenço Vander Hammen y León issued an 'aprobación' for the publication of a volume of lyric poetry entitled *Obras del Bachiller Francisco de la Torre*. Another 'aprobación,' this time by Ioseph de Valdivielso, was made out on 2 October 1630. The poems finally appeared in October 1631, the 'fe de erratas' being dated 4 October and the 'summa de la tassa' 7 October of that year.

The volume, made up of four books, is of modest proportions. The first two books contain sixty-four sonnets (divided equally between the two), eleven odes (six in Book I, five in Book II), and six *canciones* (two in Book I, four in Book II). Book III consists of ten *endechas*, and the last book, simply entitled 'Bucólica del Tajo,' is composed of eight eclogues.[1]

The poems are followed by an appendix, in the form of a letter by Don Juan de Almeida, possibly the same Almeida who was rector of the University of Salamanca in 1567–8. The letter contains translations by Francisco Sánchez de las Brozas (better known as El Brocense), Fray Luis de León, Alonso de Espinosa, and Almeida himself of some poems by Horace and Petrarch. The purpose of the translations was ostensibly to provide 'adornment' for Torre's poems. The desire on Almeida's part to 'adorn' Torre's verse was an act of generosity that suggests that he and the poet were no strangers, but the total absence of any reference whatsoever to Torre in the letter is puzzling, to say the least, and disappointing, especially in view of the mystery of Torre's identity. Neither Vander Hammen nor Valdivielso offered any information regarding the poet's life; indeed, we must depend upon Francisco de Quevedo, the man responsible for the publication of the poems, for even the name of the author. In an undated letter prefacing the title, Quevedo informed Ramiro Felipe de Guzmán, Duke of Medina de las Torres, how the manuscripts came into his possession: 'Hallé estos poemas por buena dicha mía y para grande gloria de España en poder de vn librero, que me los vendió co[n] desprecio. Estaua[n] aprouadas por D. Alo[n]so de Ercilla y rubricadas del Co[n]sejo para la imprenta, y en cinco partes borrado el no[m]bre del autor, co[n] ta[n]to cuidado q[ue] se añadió humo a la tinta. Mas los propios borrones (ento[n]ces piadosos) con las señas parlaro[n] el no[m]bre de Fra[n]cisco de la Torre ...' (p. lv).

The reference to an 'aprobación' by Ercilla, unfortunately, does not clarify matters. Quevedo indicated no date for Ercilla's 'aprobación,' nor did Valdivielso (who mentions Ercilla in his 'aprobación'), and lists of works approved by Ercilla contain no record of permission for the publication of Francisco de la Torre's verse. The first recorded 'aprobación' by the author of the *Araucana* appeared in 1580, the last in 1594, the year of his death. It is probable, therefore, that the 'aprobación' for Torre's poetry was issued within the fourteen years that Ercilla was active as 'censor.'

The first suggestion regarding the identity of Francisco de la Torre was made, according to Quevedo (in his letter to the Duke of Medina de las Torres), by his friend, the Count of Añouer. According to the latter, the author was the Bachiller de la Torre, mentioned by Joan de Boscán in his 'Octava rima.' Quevedo's acceptance of this identification is puzzling and suspect. As a widely read man of letters it seems unbelievable that he should have mistaken Francisco de la Torre's poetry for that of a fifteenth-century *cancionero* poet. And yet, with no basis other than one line from Boscán, he was able to affirm (in a second letter, 'A los que leerán' pp. lvii–lx) 'él era castellano, viuió antes de Boscán' (p. lvii), and even to suggest that Boscán and Garcilaso had imitated him in some respects. The suspicion that Quevedo was deliberately creating some kind of literary intrigue, as suggested by Enriqueta Terzano and well argued by Peter Komanecky, is not without foundation.[2] In his letter to the Duke of Medina de las Torres, Quevedo accused 'algún ingenio mendigo' of having hidden the poems for many years and of having deleted the name of the author. The identity of the 'ingenio mendigo' was not revealed, but it was strongly intimated that he was a poet; however, the fact that he had kept the poems 'le mostraua[n] ladró[n] y no Poeta' (p. lv, that is, he, the unknown, would like to be considered a poet). The inference is clear: whoever had hidden the poems was a plagiarist. The identity of the unknown 'ingenio mendigo,' 'ladrón y no Poeta' only becomes evident, paradoxically by insinuation, in the prefatory letter 'A los que leerán.' After referring to Boscán and Garcilaso's 'debt' to Torre, Quevedo went on to express surprise that Torre's verse 'no esté achacosa con algunas vozes ancianas y que después ha desechado la le[n]gua' (p. lv). Writers since Boscán had been guilty of employing 'vozes ancianas,' but only one was identified: Fernando de Herrera. Much more astonishing, however, is the affirmation that Herrera 'tuuo por maestro y exemplo a Francisco de la Torre, imitando su dicción y *tomando sus frases tan frequente*, que puedo escusar el señalarlas; pues quien los leyere, vera que no son semeja[n]tes, sino vno' (p. lvii, my emphasis). Herrera, then, so often copied and borrowed from Torre that their respective verse was almost identical, to the degree that it could be considered the same: 'vno.' Herrera was, in other words, the 'ladrón y no Poeta' whom Quevedo accuses of literary dishonesty.[3]

Quevedo's attack on Herrera may also have received a measure of support from Lope de Vega. As early as 1639, Manuel de Faria y Sousa, in his introduction to an edition of Camoens's *Lusiadas*, ridiculed the identification of Francisco de la Torre with the fifteenth-century 'Bachiller': 'Francisco de la Torre, no el llamado Bachiller con este apellido en el *Cancionero general*, como con notable engaño se dexó creer don Francisco de Quevedo, pues consta que fue conocido de Lope de Vega; i quien tuviere conocimiento de los estilos de edades, verá fácilmente, leye[n]do vnas i otras obras, que las del Bachiller son de aquel tiempo, y las de Francisco de la Torre deste, portándose cada uno conforme al que le cupo en suerte.'[4] The assertion by Faria y Sousa that Lope de Vega was acquainted with Torre is unsubstantiated and is undoubtedly based on Lope's praise of Torre in his 'Laurel de Apolo,' published in 1630:[5]

Humíllense las cumbres del Parnaso al divino
Francisco de la Torre, celebrado del mismo
Garcilaso, a cuyo lado dignamente corre.

The praise, however, is brief, and there is no evidence to corroborate Lope's acquaintance with Torre. It is the reference to Garcilaso's admiration of Torre that first suggests that Lope was also implicated with Quevedo in the latter's intrigue. If one accepts Komanecky's contention that regional pride was involved in Quevedo's criticism of Herrera (an Andalusian, like Quevedo's arch enemy Góngora), it is possible to argue that Lope may have deliberately written the name of Garcilaso (a Castilian) rather than that of Boscán (a Catalan) to substantiate Castile's pre-eminence. This view may be reaffirmed in the lines following those quoted above from the 'Laurel de Apolo':

Mas ya Febo socorre
su lira que llevaba como a Orfeo

la suya al Estrimón, ésta al Leteo;
porque pueden las musas castellanas
salir hermosas sin teñir las canas.[6]

The penultimate line clearly underlines the Castilian orientation of Lope's thought, and the final line strongly suggests that Castilian poets did not need to compose elaborate poetry dependent upon artificial devices ('teñir las canas').

The demise of pro- and anti-*cultista* prejudices permitted later writers interested in Torre's identity to pursue their investigation more objectively. In 1753 Luis José Velázquez proposed a solution.[7] According to him, Francisco de la Torre was a pseudonym for Quevedo himself. Velázquez sought to prove his hypothesis in two ways. First, he selected lines from Quevedo's poetry and alternated them with lines from Torre's works in an effort to demonstrate their similarity. Secondly, he argued that the name Francisco de la Torre was an abbreviated form of Quevedo's name and title: 'Pues si en estas palabras: *Don Francisco de Quevedo Villegas, señor de la Torre de Juan Abad*, se borra en cinco partes el *Quevedo Villegas, Señor* y *Juan Abad*, quedará *Francisco de la Torre*, con cuyo nombre quiso disfrazarse, con alusión a la Villa de la Torre, de que o ya era Señor o pretendía serlo, por el derecho que creería tener al Señorío que obtuvo' (p. xii).

No further attempt at identification was made until that of Aureliano Fernández-Guerra y Orbe (editor of Quevedo's verse) in 1857.[8] In an address to the Spanish Academy, he offered a detailed biography of Torre's life, based on documents from the University of Alcalá and on deductions made from the poems themselves. In the registration books of the university he found references to a Francisco de la Torre de Tordelaguna, and these he accepted as proof of the poet's identity. To support his theory that this Francisco de la Torre was indeed the poet, Fernández-Guerra drew attention also to the opening poem of the collection. The reference to the Jarama suggested to him that Torre was born on the banks of that river: 'Nació pues en un lugar de la ribera del Jarama; y esto, y el sobrenombre del inspirado cantor, desde luego eran indicios para suponerle de Torre-Laguna ...'[9] The imaginative weaving continues. According to Fernández-Guerra, at a tender age Torre became enamoured of a young lady of superior social status. Wishing to earn the right to approach his beloved he went off to seek his fortune as a soldier in the Italian wars. In Italy he fought on the banks of the Po and Ticino (Tesín in the poetry), but his thoughts were constantly on his lady. After many years Torre returned, only to find that his beloved – now living at the Court in Toledo – was married to a rich old man who had formerly looked favourably upon the poet. Gratitude for past kindness prevented Torre from railing against the aged husband; rather, he sought consolation in his poetry, and communicated his sorrow in poems that emphasized past joy and present sadness. He left Toledo and exiled himself from his lady. Nevertheless, 'todos los años logra verla durante la estación calurosa en el alegre esparcimiento de la aldea.'[10] Finally, at an advanced age he retired to a town on the banks of the Duero where, after taking holy orders, he dwelt until his death.

Fernández-Guerra's reconstruction of Torre's life was accompanied also by an identification of his friends: 'Veremos en los Tirsis, Damones y Montanos de nuestro autor, no fantásticos y supuestos confidentes, sino reales y verdaderos amigos suyos ... Montano era el poético sobrenombre de D. Juan de Mendoza y Luna, segundo marqués de Montesclaros; Damón se decía el famoso Pedro Laínez ... y Tirsi, el divino Francisco de Figueroa, natural de Alcalá de Henares ...'[11]

Fernández-Guerra's fabrication, however, had little more substance than Velázquez's theory. In 1925, Adolphe Coster published an article in which he rejected the hypotheses of Velázquez and Fernández-Guerra, and presented material to refute arguments identifying Francisco de la Torre as Quevedo, or possibly as Fernando de Herrera or Francisco de Figueroa.[12] Coster, in turn, proposed another hypothesis: Francisco de la Torre was the pseudonym of Juan de Almeida, then the rector of the University of Salamanca in 1567–8. This, remarked Coster, explained how Torre's poems came to be accompanied by an appendix written by Almeida who apparently had had them in his possession. Had they not been by Almeida but had fallen into his hands accidentally, the critic argued, Almeida – like Quevedo – would surely have indicated in his appended letter his surprise at finding them, or expressed regret at not having known the author. Contrary to the custom of the sixteenth century, there are no laudatory poems by either Almeida or Sánchez. This suggested to Coster that Almeida, although wishing to see his verse published, sought to veil his identity (perhaps because he was a theologian), and that Sánchez, aware of Almeida's desire, wrote no laudatory verse and refrained from making any comment for fear of revealing the secret. Later, perhaps at the approach of death, Almeida may have attempted to erase his pseudonym from the manuscript, and added the epigraph (a palinode in prose) cited by Quevedo: 'Delirabam cu[m] hoc faciebam et horret animus nunc' (p. lx).

Some of Coster's conclusions were questioned by J.P. Wickersham Crawford, in an article published in 1927.[13] Crawford wondered why, if Almeida were the author, he would remark that he had sought some 'ornamento de algún escritor deste tiempo.' The final words implied, in Crawford's opinion, that the real author belonged to an earlier generation.

In the appended letter there were also translations of Horace's ode 'O navis referent' by Juan de Almeida, Sánchez, and Alonso de Espinosa. Crawford noted that these translators were referred to (by 'editor' Juan de Almeida) as 'tres grandes poetas,' and that they had requested ('pidieron') an assessment of their translations from Fray Luis de León. Crawford then argued that 'If the editor, Juan de Almeida, was also the translator of the ode, would he not have used the form "pedimos" instead of "pidieron"? And would it have been seemly to have referred to himself as a "grande poeta"? The translators were more modest, for they referred to themselves as "tres malos poetas" in their letter to Luis de León.'[14]

Crawford then went on to explain that Juan de Almeida, the 'editor,' could not have been Juan de Almeida, rector of the university, for the latter died before 5 February 1573. Francisco Sánchez was not made 'Catedrático de propiedad de Retórica de la Vniversidad de Salamanca' until later in 1573, and did not become master until the following year. Therefore, claimed Crawford, Juan de Almeida could not have been the one who addressed Sánchez as 'Catedrático de propiedad de Retórica' and 'Maestro' in the letter under discussion. Furthermore, added Crawford, the fact that the earliest-known 'aprobación' by Alonso de Ercilla is dated 1580 also lent support to this argument.

Crawford then argued the existence of two persons named Juan de Almeida, namely, the rector, and a younger Juan de Almeida, the 'editor,' who may possibly be identified as Juan de Almeida 'el Sabio,' as first suggested by Fernández-Guerra and rejected by Coster. Crawford did not reject entirely the possibility that Juan de Almeida, the rector, may have been the author of the poems. However, if the rector were indeed the author, Crawford believed it would be reasonable to suppose that manuscripts from the University of Salamanca Archives that contain compositions by the rector Juan de Almeida might also include some of the poems that appear in the collection bearing Francisco de la Torre's name. Such is not the case; 'none of the many compositions ... bears the slightest relationship to any of the poems included in the volume of Francisco de la Torre.'[15]

In 1941, Narciso Alonso Cortés published details of a lawsuit that took place in Valladolid in 1551 between a certain Doña Catalina Perrote and a Bachiller Francisco de la Torre.[16] Alonso offered no concrete evidence to identify the 'bachiller' as the poet; he drew attention to the possibility. According to the lawsuit Torre was thirty-one years old, 'poco más o menos.' Alonso contended that this phrase could indicate a discrepancy of ten years or more, and that, consequently, it would have been possible for Garcilaso to have praised the young poet. Nevertheless, his argument is highly conjectural, especially when it is recalled that Garcilaso made no reference to Torre in his verse or known correspondence.

The latest critic to investigate Torre's identity is Jorge de Sena, whose monograph *Francisco de la Torre e D. João de Almeida* appeared in 1974.[17] This book is a detailed analysis of all the previous theories surrounding Torre's anonymity and an examination of the possible literary relationship between Francisco de la Torre and Juan de Almeida. Following some considerations of the content and style of Torre's verse, Sena carefully traces the references to Almeida and his poetry in various manuscript collections of the Golden Age. He makes pertinent observations on those poems attributed to Almeida, and on a few he feels are attributed or attributable to Torre. He concludes that, although there is much similarity in the verse of the two, Francisco de la Torre is not the pseudonym of Almeida. On the contrary he proposes another name, that of Miguel Termón, a member of Almeida's household. Sena's argument in favour of Termón is persuasive but not conclusive. The fact that both Almeida and Fray Luis de León refer to Termón as a poet whose death is to be lamented and that none of his poems has come down to us may be explained, in Sena's opinion, if Termón used the name Francisco de la Torre. Because Almeida was Termón's mentor, Almeida's possession of the poems and his request that Sánchez add his poetic homage would therefore be quite plausible. Furthermore, it would be a great coincidence, argues Sena, that 'no grupo salmantino, houvesse dois grandes poetas igualmente misteriosos, um celebrado na sua morte por Almeida, Fr. Luis e o Brocense, e outro que nenhum deles refere em suas obras e cujas composições se reuniram em volume sob a égide deles todos.'[18]

Unfortunately, the manuscript that Quevedo claims was sold to him 'con desprecio' by a bookseller is lost, so that we have only Quevedo's word regarding the identity of the poet. It is unfortunate that Quevedo did not reveal where he had come across the manuscript, nor at what time, nor did he offer any other details that might be of assistance to researchers. Indeed, there are so many omissions or irregularities in Quevedo's two introductory letters that they pose many questions and offer no satisfactory answers.

Given Quevedo's convoluted arguments to portray Herrera as a literary plagiarist, it is feasible that the name Francisco de la Torre may have been fabricated (possibly based on an abbreviation of Quevedo's full title, as argued by Velázquez). But what would have been gained by doing so? There appears to be no obvious advantage other than the weak association with the

'Bachiller de la Torre' mentioned in Boscán's poem. And if the name were that of Miguel de Termón there would appear to be no reason to alter it, since the works of Termón, a Castilian, would be equally appropriate as an example to counter those of *gongoristas*. In the same year that he published Torre's poetry, Quevedo also edited that of Fray Luis de León without any attempt to conceal the author's name. Why, therefore, alter Termón's or any other writer's name to that of Francisco de la Torre in order to prove his Castilian identity or to show that he predated Herrera? Rather than alter the author's name to suit the association with the fifteenth-century 'Bachiller de la Torre,' it seems more likely that Quevedo tried to take advantage of the name he saw on the manuscript – Francisco de la Torre – in order to mount his attack on Herrera.

Of course, it has been argued that Francisco de la Torre was a pseudonym. But this argument leads to another question. Why should anyone, Almeida or Termón, for example, have used the name 'Francisco de la Torre' when there were others of that name in Salamanca at that time, as I shall show shortly? And if Termón was *known* as a poet by Almeida, Fray Luis, and El Brocense, would it not seem likely that they would have made reference to his pseudonym, if he used one?

Some of the difficulties concerning the identity of Francisco de la Torre might have been clarified if any of his poems that appear in the collection edited by Quevedo had turned up in other manuscripts, for example, the *Cartapacios salmantinos*. The fact that none has been found suggests strongly that the poet did not circulate them, in which case not only would these poems be unknown to contemporary writers but the literary pursuits of the author would also, in all probability, have remained hidden.

Curiously, Quevedo does not refer in either of his letters to the Duke of Medina de las Torres or to 'los que leerán' to the title of Bachiller that precedes Francisco de la Torre's name (nor do Vander Hammen and Valdivielso in their 'aprobaciones'). Nevertheless, it seems most unlikely that he would have added the academic rank on his own initiative, even to fit in with the fifteenth-century 'Bachiller de la Torre'; it is more probable that 'Bachiller' was already in the title of the manuscript (the first page of the text also contains the academic title: 'Versos líricos / y / Bucólica del Tajo / del Bachiller Francisco de la Torre').

Another curious aspect of Quevedo's introductory letters is the lack of any reference to Juan de Almeida's letter appended to the volume (the letter is also ignored or overlooked by Vander Hammen and Valdivielso). Would Quevedo, by drawing attention to Almeida's letter, endanger his argument that Torre predated Boscán and Garcilaso? The references to Sánchez and

Fray Luis would surely cause any serious reader to doubt Quevedo's assertions. But why then include the letter at all?

Almeida's appendix, unfortunately, proves no more enlightening than Quevedo's introduction. The fact that Almeida makes no comment on the verse or the author is most surprising, especially since he clearly considered the poems worthy of the homage of such an eminent man of letters as Sánchez. It has been suggested that Almeida knew the identity of the author but refrained from naming him in accordance with the author's wishes. But why, then, does Almeida at least not praise the poems, and why does he not explain that the author's desire for anonymity has prevented him, Almeida, from revealing his identity? There would surely be no danger to the unknown poet's identity by stating the matter.

The curious omissions suggest, in fact, that Almeida's letter is incomplete. The opening paragraph, with its imprecise reference to 'estos versos' and 'estos papeles' is very abrupt, and appears designed more to flatter Sánchez than to reflect on Torre's poetry. The request made for permission to append some of Sánchez's translations of Petrarch and Horace was evidently granted, the translations appearing on pages 182–97 (a translation of a sonnet by Dominico Veniero is inserted on page 195). On pages 197–9, translations of Horace's ode, 'O navis referent,' by Almeida himself, Sánchez, and Alonso de Espinosa, suddenly appear without explanation.

The letter continues on page 200 but the format of the first paragraph (consisting of but four lines) is puzzling. First, the third person address is unexpected after the first person of the opening paragraph. Secondly, the 'referidos,' although referring to Almeida, Sánchez, and Espinosa, suggest an earlier identification, which does not occur other than in the names preceding each of the translations of 'O navis referent' (pages 197–9). Thirdly, would Almeida have included himself as a 'tan grande poeta,' a point strongly argued by Crawford? In the brief letter that the three translators sent jointly to Fray Luis (page 200), requesting that he judge their efforts, they modestly call themselves 'tres tan malos poetas.'

Fray Luis's reply, on pages 200–1, eschews judgment and offers instead his own version of the same Horatian ode. Following this, Almeida's letter apparently continues, the content now dealing with the propriety of using tmesis, a device that Fray Luis used in his translation. This section again gives rise to questions. Almeida defends the use of tmesis, 'elegancia aborrecida de los deste tiempo,' and cites Horace, Ariosto, and Fray Luis as authorities. However, would it be expected that Almeida defend Fray Luis's use of tmesis in his version of 'O navis referent' by including his ode 'Quan descansada vida' as one of the models? And since tmesis is the point discussed, and apparently so little used, is it not strange that Almeida should not have alluded to examples by Torre, whose very poems ostensibly precede these translations?

The conclusion drawn from reading the appended letter is that it does not hang together well. The abrupt beginning, the complete lack of praise for the poems or any reference, however oblique, to the poet's relationship with Almeida, Sánchez, or Fray Luis, suggest that the letter is either incomplete or not related to Torre. The argument that Almeida may have acceded to the author's wish to remain anonymous should not have prevented him from commenting on the quality of the verse. And if indeed the author were unknown to Almeida, it is curious that he should not comment on or express regret about the anonymity of the author. The brief paragraph on page 200, referring to the 'tres tan grandes poetas,' does not appear to belong to Almeida, and the passage following Fray Luis's translation (that is, that dealing with tmesis) seems to have strayed considerably from the stated object of 'adorning' Torre's poems with Sánchez's translations. The inevitable question that arises from the vague and inconsistent nature of this appendix is: what proof is there that this letter has anything to do with the poetry preceding it in the volume? The conclusion must surely be that there is no proof. And of the several copies of the letter that exist in the *Cartapacios salmantinos*, not one authorizes its association with Torre's verse. How the letter came to be appended to the collection cannot, of course, be explained. It presumably was included with the manuscript that had been approved by Ercilla, but since the manuscript is lost and there is no record of Ercilla's 'aprobación' for Torre's work, we are no closer to solving the mystery.

My investigations in the archives of the University of Salamanca have not resulted in my being able to identify the poet, but I have been able to establish the presence at the university at approximately the right time of more than one person named Francisco de la Torre. Unfortunately, these names, which appear in the Registration Books ('Libros de matrícula'), provide no clue as to whether any of them was a poet:

1551–2: in the section 'Estudiantes, artistas y filósofos' (folio 61b), Francisco de la Torre.

1552–3: under 'Doctores y maestros y licenciados desta universidad' (folio 10), Fray Francisco de la Torre, artysta. He belonged to the Monasterio de la Santísima Trinidad, and his name appears in the Registration Books of the next four years.

1557–8: under 'Canonistas: estudiantes canonistas y bachilleres' (folio 20), Francisco de la Torre de Tordelaguna. The name appears again in the Registration

Books for 1558–9 (folio 22b) and 1559–60 (folio 15b). There is no reason to doubt that this Francisco de la Torre is the same student whom Fernández-Guerra claimed to be the poet. It should be noted that, according to the Registration Books, Francisco de la Torre de Tordelaguna terminated his studies at the University of Alcalá in 1556, as 'Bachiller canonista.' That he should then have proceeded to Salamanca to continue his studies is entirely possible.

1559–60: under 'Canonistas: estudiantes y bachilleres canonistas,' (folio 14b), Francisco de la Torre, b[achiller] c[anonista].

1560–1: under 'Gramáticos: estudiantes gramáticos' (folio 77b), Francisco de la Torre, n[atur]al de mo[n]leral del ob[is]pado de Salamanca.

Clearly, it is tempting to look on one of the above as the author of the frequently praised collection of poems, especially since the names appear in the university registers at an approximate time when Torre may have begun to compose his verse. In view of the fact that 'del *Bachiller* Francisco de la Torre' appears as part of the title page (my emphasis), one might justifiably wonder whether Fernández-Guerra might not have been correct in identifying the poet as a native of Tordelaguna (although his biography is still unfounded). Torre's identification as a 'Bachiller canonista' might also conceivably explain both his reluctance to publish his verse and his palinode in prose that Quevedo found on the first page of his poems: 'Delirabam cu[m] hoc faciebam, et horret animus nunc' (p. lx). The names, of course, also suggest that there is little need to pursue a pseudonym, and that further investigations in the archives of the University of Salamanca may yet unearth concrete references relating one of the names with the poems.[19]

TORRE'S POETRY: A HISTORICAL PERSPECTIVE

Quevedo's decision to publish Francisco de la Torre's poetry was inspired partly by the quality of the verse itself, and partly by Quevedo's wish to counteract the proliferation of *culteranismo* (the same objective had spurred him to publish Fray Luis de León's verse in the same year). In his letter to the Duke of Medina de las Torres, Quevedo praised Torre as an 'esclarecido y docto escritor' (p. lv), 'grande ingenio' (p. lvi), whose name had been unjustly erased from the manuscript that he had purchased. Torre's poetry, continued Quevedo, is marked by 'la grandeza de su estilo y lo magnífico de su dició[n]' (p. lvi) and by his clear thinking, so that 'parece está floreciendo [h]oy entre las espinas de los que martirizan nuestra habla confundiéndola' (p. lvi). In a second letter, addressed 'a los que leerán,' Quevedo drew attention to the 'bla[n]dura' and 'facilidad' of Torre's poetry, qualities that were undoubtedly attractive to such a vehement opponent of *culteranista* writers as was Quevedo. His admiration for Torre was clearly seconded by Vander Hammen, who remarked enthusiastically in his 'aprobación': 'La obras que escriuió en verso castellano Francisco de la Torre ... no sólo las juzgo por merecedoras de comunicarse a la luz comú[n], sino por dignas de ladearse con las de aquellos célebres varones q[ue] veneramos por Príncipes de la Poesía Castellana. Están escritas con la verdad, propiedad y pureça que pide nuestra lengua, cosa singular en estos tiempos' (p. lii). Ten years later, Faria y Sousa elevated Torre almost to the level of Garcilaso: 'A todos venció el alto, dulce y feliz Garcilaso. Compite con él Francisco de la Torre, que se le siguió ...'[20]

Torre's merits were also recognized in the eighteenth century. Leandro Fernández de Moratín, in a letter dated 8 January 1788, averred that 'en cuanto al mérito de estas poesías, sólo hay que decir que su autor, sea quien fuese, es uno de los que más ilustraron los últimos años del reinado de Felipe II ...'[21] A few years later Manuel José Quintana submitted Torre's verse to a much more detailed analysis. He considered the poems to be contemporary with those of Fray Luis de León, and 'de los frutos más exquisitos que dio entonces nuestro Parnaso.'[22] Torre's greatest attributes, continued Quintana, were 'sencillez de la expresión, la viveza y ternura de los afectos, la lozanía y amenidad risueña de la fantasía.'[23] Quintana was very much impressed by Torre's ability to express his feelings in relation to the natural world: a turtle-dove, a stag, an isolated tree trunk. No poet surpassed Torre in this, Quintana affirmed. All was not perfect, however, and Quintana also observed defects in the poetry. There were a certain lack of elegance and a tendency towards prosaic expressions. And 'a veces la locución se manifiesta obscura por dislocaciones u omisiones de expresión, acaso hijas del descuido y corrupción de los manuscritos.'[24] Finally, there were in the eclogues a lack of diversity and an inability to capture the 'arte del diálogo' which resulted in 'descripciones uniformes y prolixas, que al fin cansan y fastidian.'[25]

George Ticknor, the first noted American student of Spanish literature, was enthusiastic in his admiration, esteeming Torre's poetry as 'one of the best volumes of miscellaneous poems in the Spanish language ... They [the poems] are not unworthy of the genius of any poet belonging to the brilliant age in which they appeared.'[26] According to FitzMaurice-Kelly, 'Torre merece alabanza, tanto por sus fieles transcripciones como por sus poesías originales, galantes, tiernas y sentimentales ... En la perspectiva literaria Torre aparece como una segunda edición de Garcilaso, con sus puntos de vista personales.'[27] Angel Custodio Vega underlined Torre's association with the School of Salamanca, and echoed the opinions of Quintana and Fitz-maurice-Kelly in his assessment of the poetry: 'La Torre ... es dulce y sencillo, tierno y delicado en sus sentimientos ... Es de la familia de Garcilaso ... Le falta ordinariamente nervio y movimiento, es un temperamento profundamente tímido, apocado, melancólico ... Los temas son siempre de gran ternura y delicadeza; una cierva herida, una tórtola solitaria, un pajarillo a quien han quitado el nido, una rama desgajada ...'[28]

Although Manuel de Montoliú linked Torre to the School of Salamanca (in his opinion, 'el poeta más ilustre de esta escuela, después de su máximo representante [Fray Luis de León], es Francisco de la Torre'), he was the first to question the simplicity that had attracted earlier critics.[29] 'Bien examinada su cara poética,' stated Montoliú, 'échase de ver que esta sencillez y esta naturalidad son puro producto de una refinada ciencia retórica, un reflejo sabiamente disimulado de la afectación sentimental de un alma falta de nervio lírico.'[30] Montoliú's comment that Torre's simplicity was deceptive (although asserted without examples) was substantiated to some degree by Agustín del Campo in an article on *plurimembración* in Torre's verses,[31] and by Dámaso Alonso who, following on del Campo, briefly discussed some of the poet's stylistic devices: 'Eso de la "sencillez" es mucho más complicado de lo que podrían imaginar el Siglo XVIII y el XIX' concluded Alonso.[32] Finally, in 1974, Jorge de Sena, for whom Torre 'é um dos maiores nomes da poesia espanhola do século XVI,'[33] also broke away from the traditional assessments, affirming principally on the basis of what he considered to be Torre's pronounced eroticism that he 'é menos Garcilaso do que se tem julgado ... um poeta que ... é pessoalmente original mesmo quando imita, e oferece fascinantes aspectos de peculiar originalidad.'[34]

Since the comments of Quevedo and Vander Hammen, praise for the poetry has been normal albeit in oversimplified and misleading terms. Three basic factors emerge from the generalizations: (1) Torre's poetry is very closely related to that of Garcilaso; (2) the language is characterized by simplicity of expression; and (3) Torre belongs to the School of Salamanca.

Through an examination of both content and style, I hope to show that Torre was not a mere follower of Garcilaso and that the simplicity of his style is relative. (Whether Torre belonged to Salamanca cannot be resolved, as we shall see, although it may be argued that his verse does show some affinity with that associated with the university town in the second half of the sixteenth century.) I shall try to go beyond Dámaso Alonso and Sena and demonstrate that Torre, instead of looking back towards Garcilaso and his contemporaries, is already anticipating – especially in his stylistic technique and in his view of nature – the attitude of the seventeenth century. It was perhaps Torre's misfortune that he was writing during a period of extraordinary activity and very high literary quality. His undoubted talent has therefore been obscured by the remarkable verse of such poets as Fray Luis de León, San Juan de la Cruz, Lope de Vega, and Góngora. But he is, in his own right, a poet of more than passing interest and an important transitional figure in the poetic trajectory of the Golden Age.

I

Love

In sixteenth-century Spain, poetic expressions or analyses of love reflected increasingly the enormous influence of Italian and classical verse which provided a rich and much-needed infusion to the native *cancionero* tradition. This 'new' literature, embodied above all in the work of Petrarch, found fertile soil in Spain and, thanks to the genius of Garcilaso, opened to Spanish poets a variety of new verse forms, new metres, and a new language and imagery. These innovations, despite some spirited opposition from such poets as Castillejo, found wide acceptance in Spain because the *cancionero* tradition had degenerated into virtuosity, and the use of trite, stereotyped images and overworked forms. Furthermore, the fact that Petrarchan imagery shared a common Provençal background with that of *cancionero* verse facilitated its entry into Spain. When Petrarch and his followers talked of the arms of love or the torments they suffered, they were working with material with which the *cancionero* poets were acquainted. New material added to the familiar was therefore more readily accepted. The result was a kind of poetic transfusion whereby the old imagery acquired new vigour.

Further enrichment was provided, too, by the increased dissemination of Platonism, as interpreted and popularized by Ficino, Bembo, Castiglione, and Ebreo. Platonism or Neo-Platonism not only provided poets with a philosophic basis for their analysis of love, but also permitted them to see the relationship between the lover and his beloved in a new light. In a sense Neo-Platonism authorized the adoration of the lady, since by paying homage to a being who was a reflection of divine beauty, the poet could argue that he was also praising the beauty of God.

Since Ficino considered Petrarch a Platonist, the fusion of courtly Petrarchism and Neo-Platonism was aided to a large degree by his commentaries on Petrarch and Plato. Partly as a result of these commentaries, and partly because the vocabulary that Petrarch had used lent itself well to the praise of woman's divine nature, other writers, such as Ebreo and Castiglione, frequently described the symptoms of love in literary terms with which any courtly-Petrarchan poet would be familiar.[1]

The result is that it is often difficult to determine whether a poet is expressing courtly-Petrarchan or Neo-Platonic concepts. Is he a Neo-Platonist, for example, if he calls his lady 'divine' or 'image of beauty'? Or is he courtly-Petrarchan if he talks of the arrows of love that cause him the paradoxical joy of suffering? Merrill's seminal article on Petrarch showed how un-Platonic the Italian poet's feelings were towards his Laura, and M.J. Woods has argued convincingly that Garcilaso's 'Egloga primera' was a good example of Neo-Platonic rhetoric rather than a profound adherence to Neo-Platonic ideas[2] Similarly the use of courtly-Petrarchan language will not always signify feelings that are fundamentally physical.

Apart from a few poems (some five odes dealing with the changeability of fortune and showing something of the influence of Horace, two conveying the poet's thoughts on the Golden Age and *Carpe diem* themes respectively, and one sonnet, 21/1, lamenting the death of a dog in a hunt), Francisco de la Torre's principal topic is love. In discussing his treatment of love, I shall indicate what seems to me to be the Neo-Platonic and courtly-Petrarchan elements and demonstrate that Torre's Neo-Platonism is frequently more apparent than real, and that on occasion courtly Petrarchism can serve as the basis of a Neo-Platonic concept. I shall try to show that, in fact, Torre's verse belongs more to the courtly-Petrarchan tradition than is generally realized, but that the erotic quality of his poetry is more restrained than has been argued recently by Sena.[3]

NEO-PLATONISM

For the Neo-Platonist the supreme expression of love was love of God. The essential factor was love, and at its most earthly level this was found between man and woman. If love was a common factor between God and man and woman, then it was but a short step, following the Platonic-Diotiman ladder, to seeing love for woman as a stepping stone to love for God. And the contemplation of the beauty of the beloved was the process by which man became aware of the beauty of others, of the world, and of its harmony. This led to a knowledge of the beauty of the universe and, finally, absolute beauty, which was God. In short, the visible world, starting with the beloved, was a reflection of the invisible, eternal world, and uniting them was the power of love.

This philosophical principle, however, did not appear to have great interest for Spanish poets of the sixteenth century, perhaps because of its abstract nature and the lack of centres where the ramifications of love were widely discussed (as they were in Italy), and perhaps because it is difficult for a man who professes love for a woman to keep that love on a purely platonic level.[4] To be sure, sixteenth-century Spanish verse is replete with references to the beloved – such as 'imagen de hermosura,' 'resplandor divino,' and 'angélica belleza' – but these are often poetic expressions that, in the hands of poets of limited talent, served only to expand rhetorical language and rapidly became conventional.

Numerous references to the divinity of the lady are to be found in the poems of Francisco de la Torre, and one must accept that on many occasions he was merely following a well-trodden path, the 'clichés de encarecimiento colhidos de sugestão neo-platónica,' as Sena succinctly puts it.[5] Thus, for example, in Eclogue 2, stanza 14, Tirsi refers to his Filis as 'divina y soberana'; in Eclogue 5, stanza 30, we read of 'la ninfa celestial.' Certainly it would be absurd to suggest that such declarations – repetitive and lacking any qualitative value – reflect a genuine conviction of the shepherdesses' (or nymphs') divinity.

Such avowals of divinity, however, are not limited to brief declarations. Sonnet 11/1 offers a more detailed examination of the beloved's godlike qualities. She is

El ídolo puríssimo que adoro,
deidad al mundo y en el cielo diosa,
...

el ébano, marfil, nieue, ostro, oro,
la púrpura, coral, jacinto y rosa,
passando por mi vida [sic] deseosa,
de invidia mata del Olimpo el coro.
  Yo que de la visión diuina y rara,
qual nunca vieron ojos soberanos,
a no dudar de su deydad aprendo,
  si yerro en adorar su lumbre clara,
desengáñeme amor, que con humanos
ojos por bien mi solo engaño atiendo.

For Sena this sonnet represents 'neo-platonismo de melhor,'[6] and he bases his argument principally on the contrast between 'ojos soberanos' and 'humanos ojos.' Clearly we have no mere passing reference to divine attributes here, but a 'declaration of faith' and a eulogy of the qualities that have led the poet to his conclusion. Torre commences with the 'declaration of faith,' emphasized by the superlative 'puríssimo' and the repeated assertions of the lady's godlike nature: 'ídolo,' 'deidad,' 'diosa.' He then proceeds to the metaphoric beauty of the beloved (lines 5 and 6), and from this has come an awareness of her divine qualities: 'a no dudar su deydad aprendo.' Neo-Platonic elements – the adoration of the poet, the implied passage from the physical to the spiritual – are present, yet certain factors do detract from the Neo-Platonic content. First, the poet's affirmation is much weakened by the element of doubt expressed by the 'yerro' and 'engaño' of the final tercet. The three lines contrast strongly with the positive assertions of the two opening lines of the poem and the categorical 'a no dudar' (line 11), and suggest that love is but an illusion, an 'engaño.' The poet, having developed the idea of the lady's divinity, concludes – and the conclusion is what matters – that his eyes are human and may, therefore, be susceptible to error. Secondly, and more important for the present discussion, Neo-Platonists conceived of the lady as a *reflection* of godlike beauty but did not elevate her to the status of God. In this respect, it is significant that sixteenth-century Spanish poets did not generally refer to the object of their adoration as 'Dios' or 'Diosa' or even 'Deidad.' Even Herrera refrained from addressing his 'Luz' in such terms. Francisco de la Torre, however, frequently conceives of his model of excellence as 'Diosa' (although never as 'Dios') or 'Deidad.' The inspiration for such terminology may derive from the courtly 'Dios' or more probably through association with the deities of classical mythology. It should be recalled that, in this sonnet, the beloved's beauty causes envy in Olympus, the abode of the gods; furthermore, she is an 'ídolo' and a deity with all their pagan associations. This sonnet, then, is a good example of the fusion of classical and Christian worlds wherein the adored lady evokes mythological goddesses rather than the Christian God that authentic Neo-Platonism would demand.

The deification of the lady is a common occurrence in Torre's verse, a fact that may well explain why he is so frequently considered a Neo-Platonic writer. The purpose of such declamations, however, is normally rhetorical, his way of expressing the incommensurate beauty of the beloved and of demonstrating her importance for him. Sonnet 2/1, for instance, opens with a dazzling description of Dawn ('Aurora'); the sestet continues:

> Tal a mis ojos la veldad diuina
> del ídolo puríssimo que adoro,
> Aurora clara con tu[?] paz pareze.

Inclina el Sol, inclina el cielo, inclina
los elementos, y al Pierio coro
gloria mayor que la que goza ofrece.

The opening line of Sonnet 11/1 'El ídolo puríssimo que adoro,' is repro-
duced here, and the mytholocal association is somewhat increased. Besides
the 'ídolo,' we have 'Aurora,' with whom the beloved is compared, and the
Pierian chorus whom she dazzles with her brilliance.

The combination of Christian and mythological worlds is also suggested in
Palemón's praise of his Daphnis in Eclogue 1, stanza 17, and Eclogue 5,
stanza 27. In the former Daphnis is described: 'Y tú, cuya hermosura
sobrehumana / te haze respetar por diosa eterna, / entre las soberanas
soberana, / y entre las sempiternas sempiterna.'

In the latter, Palemón, observing the 'sobrenatural beldad' of the nymph
who is singing, would consider her the most beautiful if he were not already
enamoured of his Daphnis: 'Tal era su belleza sobrehumana, / que, si vencido acaso no viuiera / de hermosura de diosa soberana, / aquesta respetara
por primera.'

The purpose of the descriptions in these two eclogues, as in Sonnet 2/1, is
not to eulogize the lady/nymph as a reflection of God's beauty, but to either
express in hyperbolic terms her superiority over other figures of exceeding
beauty or underline her significance for the lover. Thus in Eclogue 1, above,
the assertion of the first two lines is followed in lines 3 and 4 by two comparisons. There are, then, other 'diosas soberanas' whom Daphnis exceeds in
splendour. In Eclogue 5, above, the 'belleza sobrehumana' of the nymph is
again presented only to demonstrate Daphnis's superiority.

The presence of mythological elements in the quoted selections reveals the
diffusion of the classical spirit in Torre's verse and should not be confused
with Neo-Platonism. In the world that Torre has in mind there is no connection between his lady and God but only a reflection of the classical ideas of
polytheistic realms. (The comparisons also recall the fact that in mythological tales the beauty of a rival was often a source of contention among the
goddesses.)

There are, nevertheless, instances that do demonstrate a more clearly
Platonic/Neo-Platonic prevalence. (Platonic in that Torre sees a reflection of
the Idea rather than God, Neo-Platonic in that woman is the object adored.)
These instances are few, as Sena has also shown, the most outstanding being
expressed in Sonnets 24 and 28/1 and Sonnet 23/II.

Sonnet 24/1 offers the most complete assertion of the beloved's divine
qualities, although a modern reader may find in it a certain lack of warmth
because of its very abstraction and absence of concrete imagery:

Soberana beldad, estremo raro
del alma, conocido por diuino;
al exterior sentido peregrino,
y al interior por sobrehumano claro.

   Si de vuestro sin par valor declaro
lo que el alma me dize de contino,
poco bien tiene el cielo cristalino
si al soberano vuestro le comparo.

   El alma os reuerencie, que os entiende,
que del velo mortal diuina Idea
no es gloria para vos la reverencia.

   Que quien como deidad no os comprehende,
aunque de lo possible que desea,
con no entenderos niega vuestra essencia.

The emphasis on the spiritual tone of the poem is immediately evident in the first two lines. The beauty referred to is that of the soul and is divine by nature. Those who look at the lady with their corporeal senses, the 'exterior sentido,' will see only the beauty of the body, the 'peregrino,' subject to time and death; those who look with their spiritual senses, the 'interior (sentido),' will witness the beauty that is 'sobrehumano.' The soul, the poet continues, constantly reminds him of his beloved's 'sin par valor.' This eulogy is reinforced by the declaration of the lady's superiority over the sky (lines 7 and 8). The inference is clear. The sky, which is significantly 'cristalino,' or immaculate, is beyond human touch and completely divorced from the material world. By surpassing the sky the lady is transferred entirely out of the corporeal world. The soul that understands the true significance of the beloved will realize that the body, the 'velo mortal,' contains within it something more meaningful, the 'diuina Idea.' This parallels the idea outlined in lines 3 and 4. The poem concludes that anyone who has not discerned the divine nature of the beloved beyond the mortal veil has not succeeded in penetrating the true significance of her beauty, the 'essencia.'

Sonnet 28/1 differs substantially from the sonnet just discussed in that it does not describe the beloved's qualities, but traces – excellently – a process of spiritualization within the poet:

Ofrece amor a mis cansados ojos,
por sustentar la guerra rigurosa,
eterno mal del alma dolorosa,
la causa celestial de mis enojos.

Con cuyos encendidos rayos rojos,
traspassando mi vista deseosa,
hasta donde su propio ser reposa,
furiosa rinde todos mis despojos.
    Y en lo secreto de mi pecho puro
– templo a su simulacro consagrado –
de las vencidas prendas le rodea.
    El alma confiada del seguro
que su firmeza tiene assegurado,
adora en sí su celestial idea.

The process of spiritualization of love begins on the physical or exterior level ('mis cansados ojos') and progresses inward ('traspassando mi vista deseosa') to terminate on an entirely abstract level with 'celestial idea.' The fact that initially there is courtly-Petrarchan love imagery should be of no concern for, as already indicated, it was not difficult to convert this type of imagery, which dealt with the world of the senses, into Platonic or Neo-Platonic terms of the spiritual realm. The war that is fought is not on a physical level; in line 3 it is clarified as an 'eterno mal del *alma* dolorosa' (my emphasis). Nor is the lady conceived in physical dimensions; she is the 'causa celestial' corresponding to the spiritual nature of the struggle. The 'encendidos rayos rojos' (line 5) and the 'despojos' (line 8) are further courtly-Petrarchan images but again these are balanced by the spiritual element evident in 'traspassando' and the 'propio ser,' the innermost being where love finds its proper place. Having established the true objective of love, Torre proceeds, in the sestet, to emphasize the spiritual aspect of the dwelling-place. The courtly-Petrarchan love/war imagery decreases dramatically – the only instance being the reference to 'vencidas prendas' (line 11) – for love has reached its 'propio ser.' The 'pecho' where love rests is 'puro' and, furthermore, a 'templo a su simulacro consagrado.' There, safe and unimpeded, the soul can worship that supreme beauty, the source of which is the 'causa celestial (line 4), now elevated to 'celestial idea.' The struggle portrayed in the octet (with its implied movement) is replaced in the sestet by a sense of repose and a tone of thanks for the achievement of the desired goal (through such words as 'templo,' 'alma,' 'adora,' and 'celestial'), reflecting thereby the increasingly spiritual nature of the poem.

The final sonnet, 23/II, is not included by Sena in his list of Platonic poems.[7] Unlike Sonnet 28/I, Sonnet 23 does not describe a process of spiritualization, but rather evokes the lady's beauty and concludes with an affirmation of the effect such beauty has had on the poet.

La blanca nieue y la purpúrea rosa,
que no acaba su ser calor ni inuierno,
el Sol de aquellos ojos, puro, eterno,
donde el amor como en su ser reposa;
    la belleza y la gracia milagrosa
que descubren del alma el bien interno,
la hermosura donde yo dicierno
que está escondida más diuina cosa;
    los lazos de oro donde estoy atado,
el cielo puro donde tengo el mío,
la luz diuina que me tiene ciego;
    el sossiego que loco me ha tornado,
el fuego ardiente que me tiene frío,
yesca me han hecho de inuisible fuego.[8]

In this poem the physical world intrudes (lines 1, 3, 9) in metaphoric terms that are in no way limited to the material world. The delicate objects of line 1 – snow and the rose – transcend the physical in that neither heat nor cold has dominion over them. The beauty of the lady is of the same delicacy and texture as the snow and the rose but she is not subject to the ravages of time, as the remainder of the sonnet explains. Beauty is not skin-deep; the beauty that has attracted the poet comes from within, from the soul. Lines 3 and 4 confirm this. The light that comes from the beloved's eyes is 'puro' and 'eterno' for it proceeds from the dwelling-place of love, from the soul of the lady and from her eyes which are a reflection of the beauty of the soul. Lines 4 to 8 constitute a perfect summary of the theory that the external beauty of woman is a reflection of inner divine beauty. The sestet intensifies the emotion already evident in the first eight lines. Lines 10 to 13 all contain essentially non-corporeal qualities of the beloved that have captured the poet. The courtly imagery – 'atado' (line 9), 'ciego' (line 11), 'loco' (line 12) – and the strong Petrarchan tone of the last two lines complement the spiritual nature of the lady, for they are directly related (with the exception of 'atado') to the non-corporeal elements 'cielo puro,' 'luz diuina,' and 'fuego ardiente.' (It will be noted that each of the above nouns is modified by adjectives that are commonly employed in mystic poetry.) Finally, the fire into which the poet has been converted is not the one that courtly lovers suffered but the inner fire with which the soul is enveloped. The 'inuisible fuego' is the culmination of the poet's experience in the same way as it represents the climax of the poem. (In Sonnets 24 and 28/1, 'essencia' and 'idea' similarly express the culmination of the poet's thought.) The manner in which this has been achieved is excellent. In the first eight lines we have enumeration, but there is always a measure of control, since the enumerated qualities appear in alternate lines (1, 3, 5, and 7) and are balanced by the adjectival function of lines 2, 4, 6, and 8. Suddenly, in the sestet, the pace is accelerated with the appearance of enumeration in each line, increasing inevitably the emotional impact of the poem and leading superbly to the final, climactic affirmation.

The (Neo)-Platonic content of Sonnets 24 and 28/I and 23/II is undoubtedly of a more genuine nature than the avowals of divinity described earlier on pages 19–21. Torre's objective now is not to evoke feminine physical beauty in hyperbolic terms but to declare the spiritual beauty or significance of the beloved as 'idea' or 'essencia.' To that end all comparisons with mythological figures significantly disappear – there are no other divine beauties – and there are no classical allusions that might suggest such comparisons (even the term 'ídolo' is conspicuously absent).

Further indications of Neo-Platonism in Torre are of a limited nature and are restricted principally to the oft-repeated assertions of the transformation of the lover. Sonnet 32/I concludes, after describing the lady's superiority over such light-giving forces as the sun (Phoebus), the moon (Cintia), and rainbows (Iris), that none of these 'pueden causar vision de amor interna, / como la vista de mi Ninfa amada / quando en sus ojos bellos me transforma.'

An echo of this idea is also to be found in Canción 4/II, where the poet laments his misfortune. He suffers from unrequited love, although there was a time when Filis, the beloved, did reciprocate his ardour. Their love was 'vn tiempo ardor y herida / de dos almas vencidas, / cuyos pechos y vidas / fueron vn pecho, vn fuego y vna vida.'

The transformation was complete and they were one. This is, according to the Neo-Platonists, the desired end of those who truly love. The image is carried to an extreme in Eclogue 6, where Iphis commits suicide in the face of Anaxerete's cruelty. But death for Iphis is a solution in that Anaxerete will not be able to reject him and his soul, unimpeded, will be able to dwell in her body as long as she lives.[9]

COURTLY-PETRARCHAN LOVE

Courtly love was, in the words of Otis Green, 'a loftily conceived love of desire. Its moving stimulus was the beauty and virtue of the beloved, yet it was not Platonic. Desire grew in intensity and led from "pure" to "mixed" love, from sight to touch to possession.'[10] This would be the descent of which Herrera speaks in his *Anotaciones* to Garcilaso's poetry.[11] No serious sixteenth-century poet would, of course, openly express such carnal desires towards his lady, but courtly love and Petrarchism did see her, beneath the poetic imagery, as a woman of flesh and blood. Following the tradition established by courtly and Petrarchan writers, the poets of the sixteenth century sang principally of unrequited love, so that a description of, for example, the pursuit of the beloved, of her disdain, of the lover's suffering, or of present sorrow compared to past joy was a poetic commonplace. The result is that since Neo-Platonic principles could be expressed by courtly-Petrarchan imagery, frequently the only way to distinguish between courtly Petrarchism and Neo-Platonism is to view the objective of a poem or passage as a whole.[12] For instance, Sonnet 28/I or 23/II contains much courtly-Petrarchan imagery, yet the lady, I have argued, is seen as an abstract or spiritual rather than physical creature. Sonnet 12/I offers, as a direct contrast, an excellent example of the same kind of imagery but now used within the courtly tradition:

Ríndeme amor el fuerte de mis ojos
desde los más hermosos de la tierra,
y ofreciéndome paz y dando guerra,
ornan su bello carro mis despojos.

Y con los encendidos rayos rojos,
que por los ojos en el alma encierra,
tal vez mis males con su luz destierra
y tal vez acrecienta mis enojos.

Yo, de mi bien y de mi mal contento,
el que me acaba dulcemente sigo,
con las cautiuas caras prendas mías,

y es el tirano crudo tan violento,
que porque no me opongo a sus porfias,
trata mi fe y amor como enemigo.

The similarity between this sonnet and Sonnet 28/I is remarkable, especially in the first eight lines. The difference in approach, however, is evident in the first quatrain of each poem. War is waged on the poet's eyes in both poems, but in Sonnet 28 love employs 'la causa *celestial* (my emphasis) as the source of attack and the non-corporeal element is substantiated. In Sonnet 12, however, the source of attack comes from 'los más hermosos [ojos] de la *tierra*' (my emphasis) and the earthly level is never transcended but continues with the paradoxical effects of courtly love: war and peace, and the spoils of victory. The second quatrain in each sonnet underlines the different direction taken. The first lines in each are virtually identical (the 'encendidos rayos rojos'); the second lines refer to the inward journey through the poet's eyes. The third and fourth lines (of the second quatrain) of Sonnet 12, however, reaffirm the courtly context, for the result of this penetration is the uncertainty and suffering of the courtly lover, emphasized by the repeated adverb 'tal vez.' The sestet in both sonnets is definitive in establishing the different nature of the love portrayed. Sonnet 12 continues with the paradoxes of courtly love: especially the joy in the lover's suffering ('de mi mal contento'). The lover gently and uncomplainingly follows the 'tirano crudo' who maltreats him and looks on his 'fe y amor como enemigo.' The sestet has continued here with the war images, whereas in Sonnet 28 such imagery disappears once the true dwelling-place of love has been established. It should be noted, also, how the final word in each sonnet sums up the result and nature of the war. 'Enemigo' in Sonnet 12 implies a continuity of the struggle, whereas, in Sonnet 28, 'idea' reinforces the abstract level at which the poet has arrived.[13]

Sonnet 10/1 is another example of marked courtly-Petrarchan content:

Este Real de amor desuaratado,
de rotas armas y despojos lleno,
aguda roca y mal seguro seno
de mi doliente espíritu cansado,
    al enemigo vencedor amado,
rendido francamente como bueno,
de mí le siento eternamente ageno
por verse de contrarios ocupado.
    Y el tirano cruel de mi contento
burladas mis antiguas confianças
los vencedores esquadrones sigue.
    ¿Quién podrá remediar mi perdimiento
si faltan del amor las esperanças,
y si quien amó tanto me persigue?

In this sonnet there are no references to the eyes, but there are the ubiquitous battlefield of love, the arms involved in the struggle, and the spoils resulting from it. The poet has surrendered to the beloved, the paradoxical 'enemigo vencedor amado,' but now he has been replaced by rivals ('contarios'). The result is that the beloved rejects him and 'los vencedores esquadrones sigue.' Having lost his lady and any hopes of love, the poet concludes on a note of despondency. Like the final word of Sonnets 12 and 28/1, the final word of Sonnet 10 ('persigue,' so often used by Torre) reflects the mood of the poem and the poet's dejection.

In spite of setbacks, however, the courtly-Petrarchan lover would not renounce his lady or turn his back on love. In Sonnet 22/II the poet weeps and bears the chains of love; his mind is deranged, yet he is adamant: 'No, amor, no dexaré tu real vandera, / menos que con la vida y alma triste, / cantaré donde fuere tu grandeza. / ... no dexaré de amar lo que me diste.'

Sonnet 3/I depicts the paradoxical nature of love, the joy in suffering, and the willingness of the lover to continue in this state: 'Eterno mal y grato mal eterno, / a quien como contento dulce sigo, / capital y caríssimo enemigo, / quando más infernal más caro y tierno.'[14]

In Ode 6/I the poet describes his state. Love brings 'assegurados males / y sospechosos bienes.' The poet is bewildered ('sólo alcanço que muero / de no entendidos daños'). Love shoots arrows through his eyes: 'Amor en su saeta / puso yerba dañosa, / tiróla por los ojos, / dexó en el alma el yerro.' The eyes are responsible for the fire within the poet, but they cannot resist looking at the beloved, even at the risk of their own destruction. Love is an 'enemigo duro'; the senses are confused: 'No saben lo que quieren, / ni quieren lo que entienden, / que como en sí no viuen, / con confusión desean.'

Endecha 4 is addressed entirely to love, which is seen as a poison and inconsistent. Love does not seek to kill the poet but wishes to see him suffer. The result is confusion ('no sé qué pensarme'). In Endecha 5 the eyes are warned of the deceits of love ('quiere socorreros / con falso fauor'). Love offers 'glorias inciertas / y esperanças vanas.' It is a tyrant, a false friend; it besieges the lover ('Saqueó mi pecho, / dióle a vn enemigo'). And the eyes are not without fault ('Mirastes humanos / y entrada le distes').

Love is unjust, a tyrant, a conqueror, poison; it is inconsistent and full of deceit. In all this there is nothing new. In Sonnet 5/I, however, there appears a reference unusual in sixteenth-century Spanish poetry. The poet, addressing the night, remarks on the source of his suffering: 'El falso mago Amor, con el encanto / de palabras quebradas por oluido, / conuirtió mi razón y mi sentido, / mi cuerpo no, por deshacelle en llanto.'

The power of love is well documented but, of all the Spanish poets of the sixteenth century whose works were consulted, only Francisco de la Torre refers to love as a magician. A slight variation is provided in Sonnet 6/I where the beloved is addressed as 'la Maga que me encanta,' and in Endecha 9 where she appears as 'Maga fiera.' (Petrarch does use the term 'questi magi' in the sonnet 'Grazie ch'a pochi il ciel largo destina,' referring to those qualities of Laura that have transformed him. But nowhere in the *Canzionere* does Petrarch refer to love or Laura as magicians.) I do not know the source of Torre's image but it could have been suggested through association with the magical power of Medusa and Circe, both of whom appear in Sonnet 14/I: 'Esta Medusa, y esta Circe bella, / tal es la fuerça que con sus ojos tiene, / tales encantos hace con sus ojos / que yela el alma ...'

Like all poets of the Golden Age, Torre saw his lady as a source of light. She is metaphorically described as 'luz,' 'cielo,' 'Oriente,' 'rayo,' 'Aurora,' 'estrella,' and 'Sol.' On occasion she exceeds the sun or the heavens in brightness. Torre is following a well-trodden path initiated by Petrarch and imitated by every Petrarchist who knew his business.

Light-giving forces can reflect the lady's splendour. They can also be a mirror of the relationship between the poet and his beloved, in which they are combined with storm/port or cloud images that depict the relationship visibly and more concretely. Again it is Petrarch (and not the *cancioneros*) who provides the model for the wide dissemination of the storm image. Although originality had been given to it in Spain by Ausias March, the Catalan poet had used it primarily to analyse inner conflicts associated with his constant struggle between reason and desire. Despite March's great influence on many Spanish poets of the sixteenth century, Torre does not use storm imagery to portray emotions arising from the conflicts between the senses.

Sonnet 19/II is typical of Torre's approach. In the sea of his suffering ('el mar de mi tormento'), the lady (the 'lumbre clara') is his guide, but she is inconstant ('mal segura'). However, if the light disappears, then all hope is lost and life ceases to have a purpose. Death, therefore, would be a pleasant escape, but the metaphoric sea, knowing that the poet wishes death, rejects him ('y porque era matarme remediarme, / a la orilla me arroja y a mi suerte').

In Sonnet 16/II the poet, on the one hand, is enamoured of his lady but she rejects him. The result is the 'tormento.' Títiro, on the other hand, is to be envied for he can look at the storm, in which the poet is struggling, from the security of the port. Significantly, Títiro has been able to attain this security because his guiding star, the 'claro norte,' has been visible. Sonnet 19/I presents a similar contrast between the poet's misfortune and the happiness of Títiro. Cruel fate causes the poet to suffer 'en la tormenta más profunda que ha dado viento airado.' Títiro, however, can contemplate: 'el no turbado cielo / y puestos vuestros ojos en su lumbre, / passáis por el naufragio desta vida.'

Like images of storms, those of clouds may indicate the relationship between the poet and his lady. In Sonnet 2/II the poet, enamoured of his lady (whose eyes – 'dos estrellas' – exceed the sun in splendour), has been rejected. This repudiation is described as 'la escura nube del desdén altivo' that prevents the poet from finding alleviation of his suffering. In spite of his constant sighs and patience, he is unable to dissipate 'la cerrada / niebla que esconde mi diuina lumbre.' In Canción 1/I the poet's desire to see the sky cleared of clouds reveals his longing for a return to his former relationship with his lady:

No viera yo cubierto
de turbias nubes cielo que vi abierto
en la fuerça mayor de mi fortuna,
que acabado con ellas
acabarán mis llantos y querellas.

Other examples may be adduced to show Torre's adherence to the tradition but they add nothing to our knowledge of his verse.

Throughout this chapter the physical beauty of the admired lady may, of course, be taken for granted. The comparisons with goddesses, seen earlier, are hyperbolic expressions of such beauty, but they also may indicate the difficulty the poet had in describing her in mere words. Certainly verbal portraits were not common in sixteenth-century Spanish verse, and the Petrarchan prototype of fair eyes, golden hair, slender arms and body, and pale skin was the accepted pattern. As befitted a divine creature, the descriptions portray an ideal, the kind that Raphael had in mind in his famous letter to Castiglione.[15] Boscán, still restrained by the *cancionero* tradition, usually reverted to the 'no sé qué' formula, and we have to wait for Figueroa's remarkable *canción* 'Tomó Naturaleza / en su mano un pincel' for Spain's first verbal portrait of feminine beauty.[16] Torre's poetry contains nothing so dramatic. The 'no sé qué diuino' referring to Cintia's charms (Eclogue 5, stanza 21), and the rhetorical question: 'Si de su luz (of the beloved) es vuestra (of the stars) vislumbre, / y es de más perfección su semejança / ¿qué puede ser mi simulacro amado?' (Sonnet 32/II), suggest moments of descriptive difficulty for Torre.

To be sure, we do have the usual Petrarchan outline, such as the 'bellos, claros ojos,' 'cabellos de oro,' and 'lazos de oro,' but these are not, as Zamora Vicente claims, constantly present (p. xxi). There are, on the contrary, a few examples when Torre does burst into moments of chromatic exuberance that point to a marked development over the poetry of the first half of the sixteenth century. Lines 5 and 6 of Sonnet 11/I enumerate the brilliance of the beloved startlingly: 'El ébano, marfil, nieue, ostro, oro, / la púrpura, coral, jacinto y rosa.'

The metaphoric association is absolute; at no point is any physical attri-
bute isolated, with the result that we do not 'see' the 'ídolo puríssimo' (line
1), but the precious stones, flowers, and snow convey a rich chromatic
impression that envelops the lady with a radiance befitting such an adored
object. A similar approach is treated at greater length in Eclogue 6, stanza 9.
Galatea is

claro, constante y cristalino cielo,
armado de las Iris celestiales
y esmaltado de estrellas juntamente,
cuyos diuinos rayos inmortales
prestan su luz al claro Dios de Delo,
quando apareze más resplandeciente;
morada reluziente
de la rocada Aurora,
adonde muestra Flora
los blancos lirios y purpúreas rosas,
la pura nieue y el color de Tiro,
rubí, perlas preciosas,
marfil, coral, zafiro,
tesoros por preciosos escondidos
en los profundos piélagos temidos.

This prolonged description, which recalls that of Figueroa in the *canción*
'Sale la aurora de su fértil manto,' evokes a vivid colour sensation that
permits no individualization.[17] Yet there is no doubt that Galatea is ennobled
and elevated by the metaphoric association with the enumerated treasures of
nature in a way that far removes her from the delicate nymphs that people
Garcilaso's verse.

Torre does not, like Cetina, Figueroa, or Herrera, indulge in describing
the physical effects of love or talk of his inability to express himself before his
lady, but he does ponder on the acute disillusion caused by high aspirations.
Alluding clearly to Icarus, the poet remarks on his own boldness in love:
'Los cielos aspiré, cuya osadía / eternamente pago lamentando' (Sonnet
29/I). But such is the fate of those who aspire to higher things: 'pero los de
tan altos pensamientos / siempre han sido del cielo derribados' (Sonnet
26/II). The 'altos pensamientos' are transformed into 'este Enzelado altivo
pensamiento' in Sonnet 18/II, where the intensity and frustration of the poet's
feelings are dramatically conveyed by the mythological image. The imagery

of upward flight, of reaching for the impossible, and of forgetting one's own inadequacies corresponds, at the same time, with the constant declarations of the lady's divinity. As befits a goddess (with the strong mythological overtones noted earlier), the poet's (or shepherd's) frustrated desires are graphically painted through the failures of mythological figures.

The world of mythology, as is now generally recognized, is a figurative means of conveying human emotions. Mythological beings, although endowed with superhuman attributes, love and hate, eat and drink, quarrel and compose music, as do humans. The allusions to Icarus (the 'intentos / atrevidos,' Sonnet 26/II) do suggest a momentary victory, that is, in amorous terms, a physical conquest. And Sonnet 26/I details such a moment. Cleverly enumerating both the human and divine qualities of the lady (in Petrarchan and pseudo Neo-Platonic imagery), Torre concludes on a triumphant note: 'Armas fueron del crudo amor tirano / y agora son trofeos de mi triunfo.'

The fleeting nature of the triumph, however, is immediately conveyed in the following sonnet, 27/I, where fears of losing his trophy rise, Colossus-like, in his mind. Fate (the 'contrarios vientos') threatens to 'derribarme mi trofeo,' and can cause as much damage as a thousand rivals ('contrarios'), with the result that 'crece mi miedo y mi tormento crece.' This fear is echoed in Sonnet 30/I, where another classical image, that of the Hydra, is used to evoke the agony of jealousy arising from the increasing number of rivals.

The triumphant note and the admission of fears and jealousy clearly point to a love that is of courtly possession and not Platonic. The presence of both Platonic and courtly-Petrarchan types of verse in Torre's collection suggests that he was well aware of the human dilemma arising out of the conflict between the flesh and the spirit. And the predominance of the courtly strain may also indicate that Torre's natural leanings were more 'human' than Platonic, which, as Sena has intimated,[18] may not have accorded with his station in life. Nevertheless, if any such conflict existed within Torre, he does not convert it into poetic analysis. The closest he comes to verbalizing the dilemma is in Sonnet 13/I. Here the 'pensamiento altivo' is excited by his sight of the beloved, the 'cielo soberano,' who, however, having been struck by 'vn ardiente rayo humano,' flees from its dishonourable intentions ('huyó del fuego deshonrado y vivo').[19] The poet's soul regrets the actions of the 'altivo pensamiento,' which is clearly identified as base, a 'parto vastardo de ánimo liuiano.' His soul seeks the spiritual, 'los ojos,' but the beloved denies the poet sight of her divine nature ('no se precia mostrar rayo diuino') in order to plunge him again into the destructive fire of passion. The poem is not really an examination of the conflict between reason and desire, but rather is an explanation of and perhaps excuse for his human proclivities. It is almost as if the poet were casting the blame on the lady; because she does not deign to show her 'rayo diuino,' she is condemning him to the pursuit of physical desires that lead only to destruction.

The pre-eminence of the courtly-Petrarchan attitude could well have prompted Torre to pen the palinode that Quevedo reports was written on the first page of the poems: 'Delirabam cu[m] hoc fecit, et horret animus nunc' (p. lx). Such an expression of regret, however, was not infrequently a literary commonplace and did not necessarily reflect a genuine change of heart. Nevertheless, Sena suggests that the palinode may have substance, and argues very strongly in favour of a pronounced erotic element in the verse.[20] This argument is based principally on the symbolic interpretations of certain imagery, especially in those poems containing arboreal images or images of the wounded stag and of the turtle-dove. Also included within the erotic framework are those poems containing references to Enceladus, Colossus, and the Hydra (noted above), and the sea (in one instance, Sonnet 19/II). Even the night, which appears frequently in Torre's verse, is viewed as the 'noite obscura dos lobis-homens e dos vampirs, das almas paradas e dos corpos ardentes de desespero sexual.'[21] Sena's interpretation is not without merit and he has done much to correct the generalized simplifications of earlier critics, but to insist on the phallic connotation of Enceladus, Colossus, the Hydra, or the oak tree, and on the sado-masochistic nature of Torre's poetry is perhaps misleading. It is true that much of Torre's verse is an affirmation of frustrated love and that he expresses this frustration more insistently than has been recognized, but all courtly poetry exhibits symptoms of such frustration, from the Provençal troubadours onward. To describe, for example, the Hydra (Sonnet 30/I) as phallic, and the poem as 'uma confissão de castração impossível (que a multiplicação das cabeças cortadas significa),' would seem to be stretching the Freudian interpretation too far.[22]

The arboreal and animal imagery enjoys a long erotic tradition, and perhaps no other Spanish poet of the sixteenth century employs it as consistently as Torre.[23] The degree of eroticism, however, that he injects into that imagery is another matter. The maximum expression of the animal image, for example, is Canción 2/II, which Sena views as a symbolic description of the sex act: 'uma refinada celebração dos actos sexuais, da violação, do orgasmo.'[24]

To be sure, love may be the hunter that has wounded the suffering hind, but it is equally possible that Torre is merely using a metaphor, which goes back to Virgil (*Aeneid* Book 4, lines 66–73), to indicate a force that has destroyed the happy existence of the stag and the hind. (The same hunter image occurs in Ode 6/I and – with a slight variation, 'Caçador' – in Sonnet 31/II.) The destruction of a joyful relationship is substantiated in Stanza 4, where symbols of togetherness abound, but the verb tenses ('anduvistes,' 'ceñistes,' and 'ensordecistes') clearly point to a past state, which contrasts with that of the now-suffering hind. Likewise, the arrow released by the hunter (leaving the hind lifeless) need not be interpreted directly as a phallic symbol. The doe is dying of love (a very old image) and to prove her love will die alongside her beloved. It was very common for the lover, when smitten by love, to say that he was dead to himself and lived in the beloved.[25] The doe, struck by love, no longer lives in herself but in the lover, the stag, and his 'real' death, therefore, can but lead to hers. Her desire for death and union with the beloved substantiates the power of love that transcends death, and underlines her fidelity. Significantly their past happiness, stanza 4, is conveyed partly by the traditional symbol of conjugal fidelity, the turtle-dove.

Despite Sena's convictions, I am not persuaded of the phallic symbolism of the poem. There is eroticism, which is latent in the image itself, but even the erotic content is not as pronounced as that of San Juan de la Cruz's 'Canción del alma.' Certain lines or phrases – 'morirás en su seno reclinando' (stanza I), 'fatigado aliento,' 'rendir el espíritu doliente' (stanza 3), 'al agonía / de la muerte rendida' (stanza 5), 'la dura / flecha del cazador dexó sin vida' (commiato) – connote sexual feelings but they are not conveyed with intensity, nor is it their function to describe physical union. The same observation also will be made with reference to Torre's use of aboreal imagery.

The turtle-dove is the object of the poet's attention in two poems, Canción 1/1 and Endecha 7, and appears, often in conjunction with the nightingale, in several others. The tradition imposed by the literary history of the two birds – the turtle-dove as a popular symbol of conjugal fidelity, the nightingale robbed of its young (Virgil *Georgics* Book IV, lines 511–15) – scarcely permits an erotic evocation. In Canción 1/1 the poet and the bird accompany each other in their sorry: 'Yo con tu compañía / y acaso a ti te aliviará la mía' (stanza 1). Appropriately the philomel is called upon to weep for the turtle-dove ('Llórete Filomena, / ya regalada vn tiempo con tu pena'), an act that is echoed in Endecha 7, where she is joined by the wounded hind ('Llora Filomena, / cierva herida brama'). This interrelationship between the stag and turtle-dove (already seen in Canción 2/II) and nightingale might serve as a reminder of the restrained nature of Torre's eroticism.

It is the turtle-dove that accompanies the despoiled oak (Canción 2/I), a sad vestige of its former glory and an 'Inútil tronco agora / tronco pesado donde / llora la tortolilla su ventura' (stanza 3). Aboreal imagery by its very nature, can convey greater eroticism than is permitted to imagery of the turtle-dove and nightingale. However, Sena's description of the ivy/oak image as 'muito claramente, uma imagem de solidão fálica, de tenso impulso sexual,' or the oak as 'um membro viril da terra penetrando o céu, como o será celeste penetrando a terra,' seems too adventurous within the context.[26] The past relationship between the ivy and oak has erotic overtones, certainly: 'Tus amorosas ramas / ceñidas y enredadas / de la yedra triunfante y floreciente, / que reverencias y amas / de amor fueron quemadas / en la hara de su madre reluziente' (stanza 4). And the oak's present misfortune is underlined by the contrast with the rejuvenated earth: the 'licor' of the mountain stream reawakens the earth, and 'la ninfa Flora / recibe a su Menalio que la adora' (stanza 1). But again, it is the relationship with the human condition that matters, and the eroticism is refined, as if distilled by memory and time. There is no attempt to evoke or reawaken physical embraces as Herrera does frequently and so effectively, nor does Torre try to convey the actual sensation of union that transforms San Juan de la Cruz's religious verse into an erotic expression of love.

Like Canción 2/I, Canción 1/II, addressed to the oak's partner, the dispossessed ivy, emphasizes present misfortune which the poet comprehends because he suffers in like fashion. Significantly, the *commiato* of Canción 1/II calls on the *Canción* to imitate the song of the 'Filomena o tórtola doliente'; in other words, to convey to others the sentiment of sorrow that these images symbolize.

Francisco de la Torre's eroticism, then, is of a subdued nature. For him the arboreal and animal images represent primarily a concrete symbol of an inner state, principally suffering, that is caused by an external agent (usually the wind which, in the Odes, is often identified with fate).[27] Torre studiously avoids references to physical embrace, which other poets were not reluctant to make, and even in those poems based on Italian models (Sonnets 23/I and II) that contain mention of the mouth or the lips, he is careful to avoid the sensual implications.

NIGHT

For the sixteenth-century Spanish poet of amatory verse, night was generally a period when, unable to sleep, a lover would be tormented by thoughts of his lady. Figuratively, night could symbolize the absence of the lover from his beloved; it could convey, too, her displeasure with him and rejection of him. On many occasions it could underline the sorrow of the lover whose lady, the sun of his life, had died. Associated thus with the lover's unhappiness, night was conceived as an object of fear and dislike, its darkness being consistently stressed by such adjectives as 'tenebrosa' and 'oscura.'

According to Zamora Vicente, Torre 'es el poeta nocturno por excelencia en nuestra vieja literatura' (p. xxxvii), despite the remarkable eulogy to Aurora in Ode 3/I (and to a lesser degree in Sonnet 2/I) and the brilliant evocation of dawn in Eclogues 2 (stanzas 16 and 17) and 5 (stanzas 17 and 18). Nevertheless, the observation, although somewhat exaggerated, has a certain justification. Five of the eight eclogues composed by Torre open with an evening scene, and the monologues of the shepherds in these poems are delivered during the night. There is, however, no evidence of any particular attitude towards night in these soliloquies. It is, fundamentally, a temporal framework, and although the shepherds may find it propitious for the expression of their sorrow, they make no issue of the matter.

It is principally to the shorter poems that we must turn for Torre's major contribution in the use of nocturnal imagery. Although night may have a fearful aspect (for example, in Sonnet 2/I the 'espanto' is caused by the 'cerrada / y escuríssima noche' and in Ode 5/II, stanza 1, we read of the 'espantoso rostro / de la noche'), it is the positive element of night that predominates in Torre's verse. The poet finds in its silence and in the star-studded heavens appropriate objects for communication. 'Tu silencio sigo / que es callado amigo,' he confesses in Endecha 9. 'Oye mi lamento / responde a mis males,' he appeals, 'ya sabes que huyo / del Sol que has huido, / hombre convertido / en vn monstruo tuyo' (Endecha 9; 'monstruo' corresponds to the enchantment caused by the 'Maga fiera' – his lady – who has rejected him). Damón awaits eagerly the 'amiga y esperada noche' (Sonnet 7/I), and in Sonnet 4/I he appeals to the stars, the companions of the night, to bear witness to his sorrow. In Sonnet 20/I, one of Torre's most inspired compositions, the fearful darkness of night is surpassed by its positive qualities:

¡Quántas vezes te me has engalanado
　clara y amiga noche! ¡Quántas, llena
　de escuridad y espanto, la serena
　mansedumbre del cielo me has turbado!
Estrellas ay que saben mi cuydado
　y que se han regalado con mi pena;
　que, entre tanta beldad, la más agena
　de amor tiene su pecho enamorado.
Ellas saben, y saben ellas

que he contado su mal llorando el mío,
embuelto en los dobleces de tu manto.
Tú, con mil ojos, noche, mis querellas
oye y esconde, pues mi amargo llanto
es fruto inútil que al amor embío.

The stars that appear are acquainted with the sorrow of the poet, and he in turn has sung of theirs (he probably has in mind the mythological names attributed to the stars, for example, Ariadne, to whom Endecha 9 is addressed) while lamenting his own. An association is established between Torre and the stars that recalls the relationship between the poet and, for instance, the oak tree or turtle-dove. Torre does not simply project his unhappiness onto the external world but sees in the objects that surround him a potential for suffering equal to his own. The close connection between the poet and night is underlined also by the impression of protection and solicitude that night affords. The poet weeps, 'embuelto en los dobleces de tu manto,' because love, the source of his unhappiness, is not receptive to him.

The feeling of intimacy is maintained in Sonnet 15/II, 'Noche, que en tu amoroso y dulce oluido.' Night (again addressed) provides respite and makes tolerable the afflictions brought on by day. Night and the starlit heavens offer not the consolation of sleep (the normal vehicle of escape), but rather the opportunity for meditation and uninterrupted lamentation. It is scarcely unexpected, then, that the sonnet should end with an expression of hope that darkness continue.

The night that Torre portrays is not, as Sena has observed, the mystic path of San Juan de la Cruz, or Fray Luis's 'Noche serena,' and yet, in his contemplation of the stars, in his ability to see in the night a spiritual companion, there is something akin to the poetic sensitivity of the other two poets. There is no aesthetic interest in the night *per se* (except in its contrasting role with dawn); night is, as with San Juan de la Cruz and Fray Luis, a means to an end (the expression of amorous sorrow, in Torre's case).

The secular orientation of his verse renders Torre's attitude something more 'romantic,' and it is in this characteristic that he shows a development over his predecessors or sixteenth-century contemporaries. As is suggested by his concept of the amorous suffering of animals, birds, and vegetation, all the world is susceptible to love and of course to the suffering that love brings. This conception can also be expanded to include the universe if we recall that the moon and stars also love. Despite the 'romantic' element, and although Torre does not consciously or philosophically develop the idea, this view of cosmic love has as its underlying force the Platonic vision of universal love.

2

Nature

Zamora Vicente has observed that 'el paisaje de Francisco de la Torre es, esencialmente, el de toda literatura pastoril' (p. xxxiv). Torre's descriptions, he continues, are characterized by 'verdes prados frescos, llanos, esmaltados de florecillas blancas, azules, rojas. Altas arboledas ... El azul hondo, imperturbable, de los cielos ... Aguas ... siempre mansas, cristalinas, claras' (pp. xxxiv–xxxv). Although Torre's descriptions of nature do contain some elements that fall within the pastoral mould established in Spain by Garcilaso (for this is what Zamora has in mind), such generalizations are not, as we shall see, entirely accurate, and not consistent with the landscapes portrayed, certainly in the eclogues.

The function of nature in many poems, however, does follow in large degree the pattern determined by Garcilaso. Nature is employed to mirror the emotions of the lover, to contrast with his state, or it serves to emphasize the beauty and/or cruelty of the beloved. On occasions the poet appeals directly to nature, and on occasions so moving is his lament that elements of the natural world pause to listen and commiserate.

In the Spanish pastoral, particularly in poetry, the emphasis is largely on the unrequited love of the shepherd (or, on rare occasions, of the shepherdess), and there is generally no 'happy ending.' On the contrary, the poems, with their pessimism, normally terminate with resignation or paradoxical 'joy in suffering' as the predominant mood; sometimes, too, suicide or attempted suicide appears to offer the only satisfactory solution. The poetry of this period generally follows, furthermore, the Petrarchan tradition of combining an evocation of, or references to, a joyful past which contrasts with the present and intensifies the sorrow of the moment. Or, as another form of poignancy, the shepherd expresses a desire for circumstances as he wishes them to be, in contrast with the reality of his situation. In all these cases the landscape may play an integral role.

However, despite the general awakening of interest in man's surroundings – an offshoot of Renaissance man's curiosity about himself – the landscape portrayed in literary works, and above all in the pastoral, was not realistic. In literature it was the rediscovery of Virgil and Horace that offered new dimensions, especially the Arcadia of the former. To this literary reawakening was added the philosophical concept of nature as viewed by the Neo-Platonists, whereby the natural world became a reflection of the beauty and the harmony of the universe. This harmony had its source at the human level in the mutual love of man and woman, and was the result of the contemplation of the beloved. Conversely, hate, cruelty, or indifference was a source of sorrow and suffering, and each, too, was reflected in the surrounding world. These abstract human qualities, then – love and harmony, hate, and discord – were given concrete form and expression in nature by the transference of the poet's emotions to the landscape.

THE ECLOGUES

Francisco de la Torre's work includes eight eclogues, a relatively large portion of his total production when compared with that of other poets of the sixteenth century.[1] The central theme of these eclogues is that of unrequited love.[2] The shepherds bewail the cruelty of their ladies or of love but, strangely, the function of nature *within* these laments is quite limited. If we compare all the monologues or dialogues in Torre's eclogues with the soliloquies in Garcilaso's first eclogue, we will find that the use of nature in the latter far exceeds any use of the natural world in the former. In Garcilaso's poem, Salicio employs nature symbolically (stanzas 9, 10, 12), conceives it as actively responding to his sorrow (stanza 15), contrasts its unity with his situation (stanza 6), and portrays the influence of Galatea's love by means of the landscape (stanza 8). And in Nemoroso's song – the principal theme of which is the intense sorrow of the shepherd as a result of Elisa's death – nature's role is to emphasize by means of contrast the importance of Elisa's presence (corresponding to Nemoroso's happiness) and her absence (death). Not one of the uses mentioned is to be found in the soliloquies or dialogues of Torre's eclogues. Whenever nature is employed in direct speech, it is used to emphasize the shepherdesses' beauty (the amoebaean song of Eclogue I) or to demonstrate their cruelty. For example, Lícida is 'más que el Sol hermosa,' and 'más blanca y colorada / que el blanco lirio y la purpúrea rosa, / cubiertos del humor de la mañana' (Eclogue 8, stanza 11), and Daphnis is 'más intractable, más endurecida / que el mar inchado, que la sierra elada, / más que roca del viento sacudida' (Eclogue I, stanza 18).

If such is the nature of the landscape in the monologues and dialogues of Torre's eclogues, where then is their bucolic character to be found? There is no doubt that the success of the eclogues lies in the portrayal of the landscape as a background to the complaints of the shepherds, although, as we shall see, the term 'bucolic' as a general description is misleading. The landscape background is, of course, a prerequisite of most eclogues, as Doris Lessig observes when comparing the technique of the pastoral writer with that of the dramatist: 'Wie der Dramatiker in seinen Regieanweisungen Zuerst die gewünschte Szenerie beschreibt, so gibt der Eklogendichter stets eine Einführung in die Natur ...'[3]

The type of background for the Spanish Golden Age eclogue was established by Garcilaso in his Eclogues 1 and 3. It is, in Margot Arce's words, a

paisaje irreal, idealizado ... un prado verde, fresco, en primavera; está cuajado de tiernas flores ... un vientecillo suave hace mover las hojas de los copiosos árboles que ensombrecen el prado; entre estos árboles, refrescando la hierba que se enrosca a sus raíces y las hierbecillas que crecen en sus márgenes, corre un agua clara y cristalina, cuyo blando sonido se aconcierta con el dulce canto del ruiseñor ... hay un monte cercano ... Por el prado pastan las ovejas y los pastores, recostados sobre la húmeda hierba, se entregan al codiciado reposo.[4]

These observations are very much in the same vein as those of Zamora Vicente (quoted at the beginning of this chapter) when he talks of Francisco de la Torre's descriptions. But Zamora is not alone in his assessments. Early in the nineteenth century Quintana set the tone that has since dominated critical appraisal of Torre's contributions in this area. 'Ningún poeta castellano,' he declares, 'ha sabido como él sacar de los objetos campestres tantos sentimientos tiernos y melancólicos; una tórtola, una cierva, un tronco derribado, una yedra caída le sorprenden, le conmueven y excitan su entusiasmo y su ternura.'[5] Quintana's opinion has a certain justification, but it is very limited. I have already remarked on Torre's sensitivity when he addresses suffering objects of nature – precisely those listed above in Quintana's observations – and Quintana's comments are correct only when applied to the *canciones*.[6] Nevertheless, 'sentimientos tiernos, melancólicos' and 'ternura' have become generalized terms applied to all of Torre's poetry, and are, therefore, misleading. Angel Custodio Vega follows Quintana's remarks closely on the wounded doe and the turtle-dove and adds that the poems 'respiran *todas* ternura, viveza, timidez, amenidad, *frescura de campo lozano y sencillez y aroma* como de flores silvestres' (my emphasis).[7] Another critic, Segundo Serrano Poncela, affirms that Torre 'toma en traspaso el disfraz garcilasino y lo luce con *idéntico* garbo: sus verdes prados, sus blancas florecillas, sus abejas zumbadoras, las altas arboledas de robles ahogados por la hiedra' (my emphasis).[8] Such views, however, betray a hasty or partial evaluation of Torre's contributions, for there is much to indicate that he was not simply a singer of 'sentimientos tiernos' or a mere dweller of Arcadia.[9]

Let us consider the background of Eclogue 6. In this poem a destructive storm, together with a rapid change of perspective from river level to mountain height, provides a startling introduction to a pastoral poem. The initial line of the poem, with its resonant 'r' sound, sets the tone for the landscape:

En vnas yertas rocas rigurosas,
cóncabas de las olas sossegadas
de los cristales de la diosa Tetis,
por donde las corrientes sonorosas
del presuroso y cristalino Betis
entran de su furor arrebatadas,
al cielo tan alçadas,
que cubierta su altura
de blanca nieue pura
parece que sustentan en su cumbre
sustentando la blanca nieue elada,
la inmensa pesadumbre
del curso celestial arrebatada.

The Betis, then, although 'cristalino,' is hardly 'manso,' but is characterized by rapid movement and thunderous sound. The initial lack of warmth and colour is further heightened by the extremely abrupt change of perspective from river level to the tops of the waves ('al cielo tan alçadas') covered with foam. And the final two lines of the strophe, with the impersonal nature of the adjective 'inmensa' and the implied violence of 'arrebatada,' underline the sterility of the scene.

The second stanza returns equally abruptly to water level. We observe the cold north wind, which agitates the water and lays waste the countryside, and (again moving rapidly upward) the thunderbolt that strikes the mountain tops:

Turba [Arturo] furiosamente su sossiego,
deshoja y quiebra el árbol más seguro,
...

abrasa el verde prado,
altera el manso viento,
esconde el firmamento,
haze temblar la cumbre leuantada
de la mano de Júpiter herida,
de la más empinada
elada yerta sierra endurecida.

This inhospitable and harsh landscape, rising rapidly from sea-level to mountain top in a manner prefiguring baroque tendencies, is clearly distant from the pleasant river banks and shady nooks of the *locus amoenus*. If it were the only such example, it would be sufficient to cast doubt upon the generalizations summarized above. However, the background of Eclogue 5, although at first reading it may appear bucolic, also deviates from the normal pastoral pattern. It certainly does not contain the harshness and frigidity of the introductory strophes of Eclogue 6, for the watery refuge, which is 'De mil vmbrosas plantas adornadas, / quales con cierto fin, quales eternas,' is evidence of certain colour. Nevertheless, the marked aqueous nature of the first two stanzas and the sudden transfer in stanza 1 from the rock overhanging the river to the nearby sea and then to the mountains ('A los más leuantados Orizontes') allow for no development of a truly warm, idyllic picture.

The first two strophes provide us with the physical location; stanza 3 informs us that it is summer. However, instead of portraying a colourful contrast to the first two stanzas, the third stanza presents the landscape as it really is under the searing summer sun. The description is anti-pastoral in that it denies the presence of green fields, shady nooks, and gently swaying trees, yet at the same time uses much of the vocabulary associated with bucolic landscapes. The sun burns the 'florecidos campos' and 'de flores y hojas despojando / de los árboles bellos la corona, / seca los prados y las sombras quita, / abrasa el monte y el frescor marchita.'

It is, of course, tempting to see in the anti-bucolic descriptions of Eclogues 6 and 5 evidence of the poet's desire to evoke a concrete sight. Zamora Vicente (139, n. 10) feels that the opening scene of Eclogue 5, for example, may reflect something of the landscape at the mouth of the Tagus. The sense of intimacy and familiarity of the opening words of the poem ('Ay un lugar en la ribera ...') does suggest that the poet had a specific place in mind, but we also must be prepared to accept that the use of '[H]ay' was a poetic device of long standing.[10] In addition, the classical references – Glaucus, Latona, Apollo (Thetis, Arturus, Jupiter in Eclogue 6) – remind us that even if Torre is evoking a specific scene, he is doing so with his memory very much distilled by his poetic muse.[11] We have but to compare the more realistic scenes in Figueroa's *Canción* 'Cantar quiero el llorar enamorado / de Beliso' or Montemayor's first eclogue to realize how far Torre still is from a faithful reproduction of the scene.[12] We should keep in mind that the repeated allusions to storms in his odes (with their strong Horatian tone) may also have prompted Torre to include such scenes in his eclogues where, furthermore, the flexible verse form permitted him to expand upon the restrictions imposed by the structure of the ode. And yet, in spite of all this, there is still much (for example, the foaming water, the changing perspectives, the scorched earth) to suggest that Torre initially may have been inspired by a particular place. But whatever the precise inspiration, it must be recognized that Torre has stepped well beyond the restrictions of Arcadia and the protection of the *locus amoenus*.[13]

The aqueous nature of the landscape is evident in the first two stanzas of Eclogue 5, underlined by references to 'ninfas' and the sea-god Claucus, and in stanza 1 of Eclogue 6. Eclogue 8 likewise shows Torre's interest in the aquatic landscape, although the opening stanza emphasizes the arrival of Aurora in panoramic turns before focusing on the physical setting. (This eclogue is the only one written by Torre that follows the generally accepted pattern of beginning at daybreak and ending at sunset.)[14] Unlike Eclogues 5 and 6, harmony and beauty – revealed with the passing of the 'negro manto de la noche' – are evident here. The colour that Aurora unveils (for example, 'el rosicler y perlas Orientales') blends with the serenades of the birds ('pintadas aues'), whose warbling echoes through the flower-filled fields.

From the panoramic vision of the first stanza the poet focuses in stanza 2 on the 'frescura de vna cueua vmbrosa, / del curso de las aguas escabada' where the shepherd, Montano, takes refuge from the heat of the sun. Nor is the entrance of the cave without its attraction: 'Rodeada de yedra, / de juncos, cañas, flores / enredadas en árboles mayores, / ornan la tosca piedra.'

The following three stanzas continue in the same vein as the poet evokes the presence of the river-nymphs and river-god in their watery sanctuary and on the banks, and Montano is momentarily forgotten. The bucolic *locus amoenus* associated with trees, flowers, and meadows has been transformed entirely into a *locus aquaticus*, peopled by paganistic deities – the nymphs and river-god (Doris, goddess of the sea, is also mentioned) – and characterized by 'juncas,' 'cañas,' 'húmidas cabernas,' 'profundo vmbrío,' 'verdes obas,' and 'verde musgo.'

Eclogue 7, although containing fewer direct references to a *locus aquaticus*, also looks away from the Arcadian pleasance. The theme is the lament of the sea-god Glaucus caused by the cruelty of the nymph Scylla. This 'caberna' setting, therefore, matches the 'habitación vmbrosa' of Glaucus at a spot where the river Arages meets the sea. The song of Glaucus, however, follows the traditional pattern of courtly-Petrarchan complaints, but corresponding to the nature of the singer, those who listen and respond are sea-dwelling creatures and not sheep: 'Los Delphines y Phocas, con atentos / oídos, escuchauan el quebranto / del espíritu triste y miserable.' Although Cossío is to some extent justified in calling this a piscatorial eclogue, it should be recognized that the piscatorial element is limited, especially when compared, for example, with the eclogues of Sannazaro.[15] Nevertheless, that this is not a pastoral poem in the style of Garcilaso cannot be denied.

Of Torre's eight eclogues, it thus can justifiably be argued that at least four contain background descriptions that are decidedly not of the idyllic kind established in Spain by Garcilaso. This is not to say that Torre's eclogues *in no way* belong to the pastoral tradition, but I have sought to correct over-simplifications that deny Torre any originality in his works. He is not a servile imitator of Garcilaso and his landscape descriptions are not dressed in the 'idéntico garbo' that Serrano Poncela claims. Even in the four remaining eclogues Torre shows an independence that sets him apart from other sixteenth-century Spanish pastoral poets. The background of the first eclogue reveals a great deal of originality and equals, indeed perhaps even surpasses, any landscape description by Garcilaso. (I have in mind, especially, Garcilaso's third eclogue, written, like Torre's first, in the hendeca-syllabic eight-lined stanza form, the *octava rima*.) The description of the landscape contains many of the bucolic requirements: trees, a meandering river, banks laden with flowers, and sheep. Nevertheless, the scene is dominated by an almost overwhelming forest which visually dwarfs the shepherd, Palemón, who wanders therein. And the trees are not motionless but sway gently in the wind, some reaching towards the heavens and others bending in counterbalancing motion towards the river. The river banks, 'crowned' (not dotted) with flowers, add to the sensation of profusion. The result is a picture that looks to the baroque concept of nature as an omnipotent force, dominating man by its presence, rather than to the classical idea of nature as a static although integral background to the human figures. In this sense, Torre's descriptions exceed any of those of Garcilaso, and betray an interest in the landscape that may not be entirely dependent upon literary tradition.

The initial background of Eclogue 2 differs from that of the first eclogue in form, but the density of the vegetation and its unity are scarcely less evident. The season appears to be spring, as Flora and nature go about

Bordando el gentil prado
de verde y encarnado,

la hermosura de Arabia descubriendo,
los descasados árboles texiendo,
clarificando el sol, mostrando el día,
puro y sin nube qual la luz le cría.

The harmony of the picture is underlined by the gerunds 'Bordando' and 'texiendo' (implying the creation of a close relationship of several parts), and the rhythmic effects of 'descubriendo,' 'clarificando,' and 'mostrando.' The description of the activities of Flora and Natura is followed by that of the river, the banks of which are crowned by colourful flowers ('blancas, rojas y purpúreas'). The river plays an integral part in sustaining the splendour of the earth ('sustentando al prado sus colores, / con su cristal a trechos derramado'). The colour of the vegetation and the sound of the river, then, offer a picture of peace and tranquillity, and even the approaching night, with its ominous implications, causes no rupture in the scene. Stars begin to shine and the colour of eventide spreads across the earth, blending with the scene already painted. Nightfall, however, coincides with the arrival of the forlorn Tirsi, who immediately proceeds to sing of the cruelty of his Filis. The lament culminates in Tirsi's suicide when he throws himself into the river (stanza 14). Now nature, which in stanza 3 responded passively to Tirsi's complaints by a cessation of movement, reacts vigorously to the destructive act and, in a short, volcanic burst of noise, discord is created in a previously harmonious scene. The short lines, the predominance of the resonant 'r' sound, the brief enumeration, and rapid visual contrast of height and depth ('montes,' 'valles') accentuate the rapid, noisy movement of the water. At this climactic moment, when noise and turbulence dominate, when darkness covers all, we are confronted with the sudden arrival of Dawn, bringing light and colour to all parts:

Salía ya la Aurora derramando
por las azules, blancas, rojas flores,
el nectar soberano que las cría,
dando sus perfectíssimos colores
a quanto mansamente va mirando
en monte, soto, y valle, y selva vmbría.

Following Aurora, the sun appears, 'Serenando los vientos leuantados, / resplandeciendo con su luz los prados / y descubriendo en ellos la hermosura / que inuidiosa eclipsó la noche escura.' The metamorphosis is intense and striking and obeys an aesthetic impulse that points more to the baroque than to the early sixteenth-century pattern. A number of artistic contrasts are perceptible: darkness and light, achromatism and colour, violence and harmony, and movement and repose. Not here the gradual temporal transformations that were normal in bucolic verse, where, for example, the sunset, although often condensed into the final stanza, would blend with the general tone of the poem.

The kind of contrast in Eclogue 2, resulting from the sudden arrival of Aurora, is not unique in Torre's verse; it occurs also in Eclogue 5. The initial stanzas describe in turn the banks of the Tagus and a sun-scorched landscape. In stanza 17, following the lament of Palemón (made during the night) and the report of his swoon, a complete transformation takes place. Suddenly we are informed that

> Blancas, purpúreas flores produziendo,
> prados, valles, montes aljofarando,
> las sombras de la noche deshaziendo,
> los ayres y los cielos alegrando
> rompió la Aurora con su luz, saliendo,
> las negras nubes del Oriente ...

Following several stanzas in which colour plays no role, the function of Aurora is, as in stanza 16 of Eclogue 2, to provide an aesthetic and visually pleasing contrast with all that is associated with darkness and sorrow.

Eclogue 4, like Eclogue 2, opens by affirming the beauty of a spring evening. Spring personified appears, crowning the river banks with flowers, embroidering the fields with splendid colour, and regaling the trees with leaves:

> Coronando de flores la ribera
> ...
> bordando el verde prado
> con los viuos colores
> de azules, blancas flores,
> vistiendo las desnudas plantas de hojas,
> quales escuras verdes, quales rojas,
> entretexiendo el arboleda vmbrosa
> yedra con roble, vid con olmo hermosa.

The impression of profusion and density is accentuated by the general absence of conjugated verbs, which has the effect of condensing the images and emphasizing the picture created by the adjectives and nouns. As in the second eclogue, the unifying agents are the gerunds 'bordando' and 'entre-texiendo,' reinforced by two further gerunds, 'coronando' and 'vistiendo.' Having presented a general picture, the poet then focuses (in stanza 2) on a cave on the banks of the river Tesín. As befits a more aqueous environment, there is a loss of colour compared to that of the first stanza, although the cave is 'ornada toda de verbena y yedra.' But there is no loss of harmony as the third strophe assures us; this is the place

Donde la fuente resonaua,
el ayre entre las flores se metía,
los valles resonauan sin aliento,
el viento su braueza suspendía
y las yeruas y rosas meneaua,
dando a su perfección más ornamento.

In these surroundings, the songs of the 'bellas sirenas' have the magical quality of suspending time itself. It is in this environment that Tirsi complains of his 'dolor grauíssimo'; the complaint is directed not to his lady but at unjust Love. Tirsi's monologue is followed by a parallel lament against Love delivered by the recently arrived, unnamed, nymph, after which they both retire 'a la parte del valle más sombría' (stanza 19). Here the agreeable nature of the retreat is evoked: a cave protected by trees and encircled by flowers forming a pleasant invitation to repose from the heat of the sun. The picture is completed by a more detailed description of a mountain spring, the force that provides water for the 'alameda fresca' and feeds the trees. The spring's pure, crystalline quality is suggested by the reference to the 'mármoles de Paro,' the comparison with snow, the use of the superlative '-íssimo,' and the effect of the unvoiced 'c' in 'claríssima,' 'cristal,' and 'fresca.' And the picture is not a static one. After having given sustenance to the grove where Tirsi and the nymph have sought refuge (to be later joined by another shepherd), the stream proceeds 'por vnos yertos riscos empinados / del curso de las aguas quebrantados, / haziendo vn ronco son de peña en peña, / en el sagrado río se despeña.' This is not the description of quiet, gently flowing waters normally associated with the pastoral world, but of a waterfall, which conveys (as did other elements in Eclogues 2, 5, and 6) a rapid visual movement from height to depth. The impression of increasing movement is well communicated by the enjambement, and the agitation of the water and the growing noise are transmitted by the 'r' sound of 'yertos riscos,' 'quebrantados,' and 'ronco.' Immediately following this picture of increasing movement on which the poet has focused, we are returned, in the kind of contrast so favoured by Torre, to a static scene where Tirsi and the nymph are seated alongside a spring, recounting their respective tales of grief.

Zamora Vicente summarizes his discussion of the landscape in Francisco de la Torre's poetry as 'un campo quieto, en eterno amanecer y en constante primavera' (p. xxxvii). Such a conclusion has been hastily drawn, for Torre shows himself to be far less pastoral than, for example, his great predecessor Garcilaso. Indeed the very length of the background descriptions of the eclogues suggests an interest in the natural world independent of Arcadia. Certainly few, if any, other pastoral poets of the sixteenth century so consistently provide such a long and detailed background to the laments of their shepherds.

RESPONSIVE NATURE AND NATURE ADDRESSED

> Con mi llorar las piedras enternecen
> su natural dureza y la quebrantan;
> los árboles parece que se inclinan;
> las aves que me escuchan, cuando cantan,
> con diferente voz se condolecen.

With these words of Salicio (Eclogue 1), Garcilaso set the pattern for nature's response to the suffering of a lover, and Francisco de la Torre, like virtually all Golden Age poets of amatory verse, follows in the same steps. In the very first poem of Book 1 we read that the joyful singing of the happy Títiro causes the rivers Tagus and Jarama to pause and listen, and the tears of the poet find their echo in the weeping willow: 'Yo ... / cuelgo mi caramillo de vna rama / de salce y lloro, lloro y él suspira.' In Eclogue 1, stanza 9, Palemón's suffering at the hands of his cruel Daphnis is so acute and his lament so moving that 'El monte ablanda, ... detiene el río, / el cielo para, inclina el viento frío.' And so on.

Such a passive response, however, does not always characterize Torre's verse. In Eclogue 2, stanza 15, for example, the river, the only witness to Tirsi's suicide, responds to the tragic act by a notable increase in sound and movement:

> estremeciose el cristalino río
> y con vn riguroso y cruel bramido
> se fue por las riberas esparciendo
> y, del terrible estruendo

los valles resonaron,
los montes retumbaron,
hiriendo la arboleda sonorosa
de la ribera clara y espaciosa,
y, entrando por el río presuroso,
acabó de turballe su reposo.

A parallel process occurs a short time later (stanza 21), after Dórida's
self-willed death: 'Estremeciose el río embrauecido / y, resonando fiero su
corriente, / ensordeció la selua sossegada.' In both instances nature's reac-
tions are emphatic and tempestuous in accord with two basically violent
actions, and more reminiscent of Cetina's turbulent river descriptions than of
Garcilaso's static evocations.

The recognition of nature's awareness of human feelings is what Gillet
terms 'a sort of panpsychism' or 'a sense of unity between nature and man.'
Nature's response to man's suffering (and joy) is, he continues, 'possible
only on the basis of the Renaissance acceptance ... of a divine principle
immanent in nature through which it could share the feelings of humanity.'[16]
The 'divine principle' in nature may have interested theologians, such as
Fray Luis de Granada or Fray Luis de León, but it was not the concern of
the sixteenth-century pastoral poet. For him nature was, among other things,
a source of comfort and consolation without theological implications. In the
solitude of his bucolic surroundings, the suffering lover could find an ade-
quate and sympathetic response because, without the interruption of his fel-
low man, he could impose his feelings on nature and conceive its response as
he wished.[17]

Appeals by the poet (or lover) to various elements of the natural world are
evidence of the sense of unity felt between man and his world. One of these
elements most often addressed is the river, sometimes in conjunction with
the wind (as in stanzas 2 and 27 of Torre's first eclogue). This is not an
illogical choice. Since absence is a conventional feature of the lover's suffering, the desire to communicate feelings becomes an important corollary,
and the river, passing through the town or region where the beloved resides,
can figuratively convey his thoughts to her. Thus in Torre's Sonnet 8/I, the
poet addresses the 'Claro y sagrado río,' whose banks provide a respite in
his troubled life, and implores it to carry with it his grief to his lady: 'Lleua
mi voz y lástimas contigo. / Aliuia tú, lleuándolas, mis penas.' In Sonnet
17/I, the poet greets the 'sagrado y cristalino río,' swollen with his tears, and
begs it to participate actively in pacifying his lady's anger (metaphorically
seen as a 'cerco de nubes espantoso'). The appeal may also expand to incor-

porate other elements of nature. In Eclogue 2, stanza 11, for example, Tirsi addresses not only the 'Claras corrientes, cristalinas ondas,' but also the river banks and the trees. Indeed, in the following stanza, the number of objects petitioned increases dramatically to include the sky and heavenly bodies – the moon and stars – in addition to pagan deities:

Clara agua, verde prado, fuente amena,
manso aire, luna escura, valle vmbrío,
ardientes luces, cielo sacrosanto,
Dríadas bellas, Náyades del río,
compañía de Oréadas serena,
fieles testigos de mi graue llanto

...

aplicad el oído
a mi doliente voz entristecida.

The inclusion of the 'Dríadas,' 'Náyades,' and 'Oréadas' – spirits that dwell in the countryside – implies a kind of pagan pantheism and serves to remind us of the constant proximity of the classical world in Torre's verse.

A much more significant corollary of the sense of unity between man and nature is to be found in the attitude of the poet to living objects of the world. Arboreal and animal imagery has already been discussed towards the end of Chapter 1, principally the role of each as visual representations of tragic human relationships. A curious aspect of Torre's use of these symbols, however, is that they sometimes become the subjects of complete poems and are not isolated images that bear out the message of a particular poem. Thus Canción 2/II is directed entirely to the 'Doliente cierua,' with no reference whatsoever to any human element; Canción 1/I is addressed to the 'Tórtola solitaria' and Canción 2/I and 1/II to the oak tree and the ivy respectively.

The difference between Torre's approach in these four poems and in those discussed earlier in this chapter is that in the latter poems nature's function is merely to react to and mirror the human situation. This is the normal relationship between man and nature in sixteenth-century poetry, whereby the former transposes his feelings onto the landscape and, if the landscape is to have any 'life,' it is in relation to man's emotions. Of course, nature can be independent or interdependent, as we shall see shortly, or on a grander scale it can acquire the autonomy of 'Natura naturans,' but where emotion – particularly suffering – is involved, the process is usually one way, from man to nature.

Torre's simple but effective technique has been to reverse the normal order of relationship, endowing nature with emotions and sufferings with which the poet identifies. Here it is not nature that participates in man's sorrow, but rather man who feels compassion for the tragedy of one of nature's creatures and then relates it to his own situation. Torre's innovation, insignificant as it may seem, marks him as a poet of no little sensitivity; the association he depicts is reminiscent of the Romantic feeling for nature and recalls in some ways the verse of the eighteenth-century pre-Romantic poet from Salamanca, Meléndez Valdés.[18]

Canción 2/I, for example, begins with the dramatic description of the oak tree, isolated and robbed of the ivy that formerly embraced it. This state of isolation is emphasized by the contrasting plenitude and colour of the surrounding world, where mountain streams feed the plants and flowers and Flora scatters colour in all directions. There is evident harmony and only the oak is unable to participate in it: 'Tú solo despojado' (the 'Tú solo' is a significant variant from the usual 'Yo solo,' referring to the poet's/lover's unhappiness; the very fact that the 'Tú solo' refers to an object of nature underlines the new perspective). The misfortune of the oak is further accentuated by the allusion to its previous state, when it was 'la gloria / y el ornamento de la selua vmbría' and when it was embraced by the 'yedra triunfante y floreciente.' The tree, which once gave protection to those who suffered, in its turn now experiences sorrow, the tempestuous south wind having torn its beloved ivy from it. It is at this point that the personal element, the identification of the poet's sorrow with that of the oak, appears. It is in the form of a question addressed to the mild west wind: '¿qué 's de tu soplo tierno, / que tus contrarios me hacen cruda guerra?' The personal 'me' appears quite inconspicuously, but the very fact that the poet has moved, with an unexpectedness that the reader almost overlooks, from the statement that the south wind was responsible for the oak's misfortune to the question directed to the west wind regarding his own hope serves to heighten the close relationship between the poet and the tree. The abruptness of the change and its inconspicuous nature are not, however, contradictory, but underline the thinking of the poet in the poem. He has, in effect, so long associated the oak's state with his own that the transition from the address to the tree ('Tú') to the inclusion of his own experience ('me') in consecutive phrases is not illogical.[19] This technique of sudden transition is reminiscent of Horace, in which the logic for apparently unrelated associations is to be found, not in the external structure of the poem, but in the internal working of the poet's mind. (Horatian elements, as we shall see later, are not lacking in Torre's verse.)

Canción 1/ii differs from the poem just discussed in that the association between the ivy's suffering and that of the poet is here identified in the opening stanza. Addressing the 'verde y eterna yedra,' now, however, 'viuda y deslazada / de las ramas del olmo, honor del prado,' the poet draws attention to the similarity of their respective situations in the final two lines of the strophe ('Lloremos juntament / tu bien passado y tu dolor presente'). The remainder of the *canción* focuses entirely on the plight of the ivy with a feeling of compassion that is entirely unexpected in sixteenth-century Spanish verse, and that is not found elsewhere, with the exception perhaps of some of Francisco de Rioja's works, until the poetry of Meléndez Valdés in the eighteenth century. Torre has succeeded in making a small object of nature the centre of attention, and the poet's suffering is not touched upon until the final stanza, the envoy, where the poem (addressed), together with the nightingale and the turtle-dove, are requested to have compassion for his troubled life ('mi vida ansiada').[20]

In the last analysis, this picture of suffering nature is, of course, a projection of the poet's feelings, but Torre offers a new orientation that sets him apart from his contemporaries. However, it would be a mistake to see in this an appreciation or an awareness of the realities or beauty or nature; Torre is working with literary *topoi* and the framework of his new orientation remains very much literary. Nevertheless, by conceiving these elements as having a 'life' of their own, he has demonstrated an interest in them beyond their previous functions and has taken perhaps some tentative steps towards releasing them from their literary bondage.

HARMONIOUS NATURE

From what has been said it is evident that the poet is aware of nature's ability to reflect his sorrow and mirror his feelings, yet in his very appeals there is also the implication that nature can be indifferent, that it can be beautiful and harmonious, and that it can appear completely unrelated to the poet's emotions. In the face of nature's disinterest, the unity and concord of the landscape serve to intensify the lover's sorrow and alienation. Again, Garcilaso provides the model for Spanish poetry. In lines 13–18 of Eclogue 2, Albanio laments his estrangement from his surroundings as a result of Camila's rejection:

El dulce murmurar deste ruido,
el mover de los árboles al viento,
el suave olor del prado florecido

podrían tornar d'enfermo y descontento
cualquier pastor del mundo alegre y sano;
yo solo en tanto bien morir me siento.

It is evident that nature here is beautiful and that Albanio is unable to participate in that beauty. The feeling of isolation is created by the enumeration, here brief, of the harmonious elements of the landscape, followed by the dramatic 'yo solo en tanto bien morir me siento,' which produces a sudden and discordant note in the scene. Francisco de la Torre, like so many poets of the sixteenth century, follows the same pattern. Ode I/II, one of his most striking poems, is an outstanding example. We are presented initially with an idealized picture of Spring (personified in the form of Flora) who, dressed in the colours of Aurora, proceeds metaphorically to cast off the mountain 'La cauellera cana / del viejo inuierno.' It is a moment of birth and rejuvenation, of hope ('el nuevo fruto'), and optimism. This optimism is conveyed by the complete sense of harmony and interdependence in the natural world, and an appeal is made (indirectly, by means of the imagery) to the senses of sight and sound, those most vital for the appreciation of harmony. The mountain stream that nourishes the plants and flowers, whose perfume in turn is carried by the wind, is constantly in movement ('Deslízase corriendo / ... / las alturas huyendo'). Then, in stanza 4,

Corre bramando y salta
y codiciosamente procurando
adelantarse, esmalta
de plata el cristal blando,
con la espuma que quaxa golpeando.

But the stream is a source of life also, as it passes through the landscape, dressing and beautifying the world, and neutralizing the intense heat of the sun. This joyful portrayal reaches its climax in stanza 8 with the enumeration of life-giving and colour-bearing objects of nature and the appearance of the arboreal image of the elm entwined by the vine and its variant, the ivy:

Todo brota y estiende
ramas, hojas y flores, nardo y rosa;
la vid enlaza y prende
el olmo y la hermosa
yedra sube tras ella presurosa.

It is precisely at this moment of most explicitly expressed harmony (underlined by the arboreal image) that the poet excellently expresses his isolation and sorrow. 'Yo triste' is the quiet, but affirmative declaration. This world is the barren, colourless one of winter, which contrasts vividly with the proliferation of life that the poet observes around him ('el cielo quiere / que yerto inuierno ocupe el alma mía'). The effect is further accentuated by the climactic structure of the first eight strophes, where the poet makes no reference to himself. Suddenly, with the 'Yo triste' of stanza 9, the bubble of beauty is burst, and with the inclusion of the human element the reader sees the picture in its proper perspective. The isolation of the poet is emphasized too by the implication that there was a time when he was able to experience the joys of spring. The poem concludes by returning briefly to the natural world, portrayed now, however, in entirely symbolic terms. The poet appeals to his Filis that, through her love, he too may experience the same hope that he has witnessed in nature: 'Renueua, Filis, esta / esperança marchita ... / ... / Ven Primauera, ven mi flor amada.'

Although the purpose of both Garcilaso and Torre is the same – emphasizing the isolation of the lover – Torre's description has moved well beyond Garcilaso's 'dulce murmurar.' The movement of the water – so fast and noisy that it creates foam – has a fascination for Torre that Garcilaso never displays. And although the mythological references – Flora, Aurora (twice), the marble of Paros, Zephyr – remind us that this is not a realistic picture, the landscape does have a vitality that distinguishes it from the gentle surroundings of Garcilaso's *locus amoenus*. Even the number of stanzas devoted to the description suggests the marked interest that Torre had in the landscape, as if, carried away by the fast-moving stream, he had forgotten the human element. (It must be recognized, however, that the delay in introducing the personal element may have been deliberately sought in order to increase its dramatic effect.)

Despite the fine poetic qualities of Ode I/II, the most outstanding example of a harmonious landscape that contrasts with a lover's alienation as a result of unrequited love occurs in the background description of Eclogue I. The first strophe provides both the physical setting (the banks of the Tagus) and the season, spring, and informs us of the presence of the protagonist, Palemón, 'De su ninfa cruel aborrecido.' The appearance of Palemón, immediately succeeding the colour and beauty of the opening lines, is not without significance in view of the integral role that this eclogue's landscape background has in emphasizing the shepherd's sorrow. The second stanza turns to Palemón's suffering and the third focuses on his isolation ('Solo por la ribera sola llega, / de su dolor acompañado solo'). Following this, in stanzas 4, 5, 6, and 8, is a vivid and artistically excellent description of the harmony of the natural world, profuse in colour. The river bank is crowned with flowers and plants, some large, some small, some few in number, and others numerous. It is a rich, pulsating environment that, however, never appears disorderly or uncontrolled, thanks to the stylistic devices employed (as we shall see in the next chapter). There is in the interrelationship of the elements a sense of mutual dependence that emphasizes the isolation of the shepherd who stands in the midst of it. The elm tree, embraced by the ivy and the vine, underlines the relationship of the natural world, as described in stanza 5 ('Sube la yedra con el olmo asida / y en otra parte con la vid ligado; / ellas reciben de su arrimo vida / y él de sus hojas ornamento amado'). The sensation of movement – as evidenced by the verbs 'suben,' 'caen' (stanza 4), 'sube,' 'reciben,' 'se retira,' and 'buelue' – is a reminder too of the awakening of life in spring.

Further emphasis on this peaceful, harmonious background continues in stanza 6, where an almost overwhelming number of trees (myrtle, laurel, cypress, poplar, plane, and cedar) sway in unison in the gentle wind. Suddenly, in the midst of all this beauty and symmetry, and in these very trees, the Philomel, the symbol of sorrowful love, appears (stanza 7), reminding us of the underlying tension of joy and sadness in the poem. Attention moves away momentarily from the landscape, and the vocabulary reflects the predominant mood of the strophe ('Querellas,' 'gravissimo daño lamentando,' 'tristíssimo gemido,' 'canto dolorido'). The bird, although a part of nature, is unable because of its sorrow to participate in nature's beauty. The sudden contrast between the mood of this stanza and that of the preceding stanzas reminds us of and heightens Palemón's situation, for he, like the philomel, suffers the wounds of love (although no mutual recognition is indicated here). The very first line of stanza 7 ('Donde mirando los alegres prados') clearly re-establishes the shepherd's position: he can perceive the harmonious world around him but cannot feel a part of it. The burst of colour that follows is a final affirmation of the beauty and harmony of the landscape before Palemón begins his monologue. There are 'Valles vmbrosos y árboles floridos, / de blancas, rosas flores matizados, / vnos brotando y otros florecidos.'

The role of nature as a contrast to the protagonist's grief is more evident in this first eclogue than in any of the other seven by Torre. Its success lies principally in the fact that there is never a division between the landscape and the shepherd. Because the shepherd is always an integral part of the landscape, his inability to participate in nature's unity is, of course, even more pronounced. The impression that Palemón is an integral part of the world is achieved very simply: he is not introduced at the end of the land-scape description but appears, as noted earlier, in the very first stanza. He is, therefore, present, as it were, in the descriptions that follow, witnessing what the reader observes. The result is a visual impression of total integration between man and nature (visual to the *reader*, since Palemón does not feel a part of this world). In all the other eclogues (except the third, which contains no background), the protagonists appear after the landscape introductions and, therefore, remain, to some extent, superimposed on the landscape, in the same way that Salicio and Nemoroso are superimposed on the back-ground of Garcilaso's first eclogue. This first eclogue is, perhaps, Torre's finest piece of verse, where theme, style, and emotional content combine with superlative effect.

NATURE AND THE BELOVED

Since the poet's lady was the light of his life, it is scarcely unexpected that that light should cast its reflections on the world and illuminate it for her admirer. Conversely, of course, her disdain or her absence could obfuscate all that he saw and render it sterile and colourless. Such imagery was com-monplace in sixteenth-century verse and Francisco de la Torre drank of the same poetic fountain.

Nevertheless, on occasion Torre creates a beautiful landscape regardless of the absence of the beloved. Stanza 37 of Eclogue 1 begins: 'La bella ninfa Primauera y Flora / de flores cubren el marchito prado: / vna le viste y otra le colora: / vna de verde y otra de encarnado.' There can be no disputing the aesthetically harmonious result, but when Cintia arrives the splendour created by Primavera and Flora is surpassed: 'Mas no tan presto sale mi pastora / dando su luz a todo lo criado, / quando del resplandor hermoso della / cubierta queda su presencia bella.'

Likewise in stanza 17 of Eclogue 5, Aurora appears 'Blancas, purpúreas flores produziendo, / prados, valles, montes aljofarando.' But then 'otra diuina luz del claro dí / tras el Aurora como Sol salía.' The result is that 'Huyen las nubes, resplandece el cielo / del claro rayo de su luz herido, / serena el ayre, reuerdece el suelo, / vno mirado y otro suspendido.' This alone attests to the power of the nymph's presence, but that is not all. Dawn, we recall, scattered dewdrops and colour on the fields, valleys, and moun-tains; the appearance of the nymph causes these dewdrops to be converted into Oriental pearls, something even more precious: 'El nectar del Aurora, el claro yelo / en flores, yeruas y árboles vertido, / endurecida su primera forma, / en Orientales perlas se transforma.' This type of description, whereby feminine beauty improves upon an already pleasing evocation of natural splendour, is unknown to Garcilaso, but is not surprising in Torre, given his consistent references to the divinity of the adored object. This hyperbolic imagery, portraying superhuman powers, corresponds to the role of goddess that woman has in his verse.

These sketches of the landscape in relation to the beloved remind us that nature is not an object of study in itself, although as an adjunct to the feelings of the poet or the lover it is never far away. The general tenor of Torre's descriptions of nature may be viewed as pastoral, but there are significant deviations that point away from the tranquillity associated with bucolic scenes. The violence at the beginning of Eclogue 6, the aridity of the earth in Eclogue 5, and the marked interest in the *locus aquaticus* in Eclogues 7 and 8 amply demonstrate Torre's contribution to the Spanish pastoral.

Torre's landscape descriptions also differ from those of other sixteenth-century poets in that they contain a great deal more movement than has hitherto been recognized. The rapid passage of water, which seems to have a special attraction for Torre, is remarkable for a pastoral poet. In such descriptions he far surpasses Cetina, a poet more normally associated with river scenes. Except for Eclogue 1, where the Tagus scarcely moves, the rivers or streams are characterized by such expressions as 'se apresura' (Eclogue 2, stanza 1), 'impetuoso corre resonando' (Eclogue 2, stanza 2), 'presto curso' (Eclogue 4, stanza 2), 'haciendo vn ronco son' (Eclogue 4, stanza 20), 'corre tan vfano' (Eclogue 5, stanza 1), 'presuroso' (Eclogue 6, stanza 1), and 'presuroso y presto curso' (Eclogue 8, stanza 3). The effect of water upon stone is more than once brought to our attention (Eclogue 4, stanza 2; Eclogue 5, stanza 2; Eclogue 6, stanza 1; and Eclogue 8, stanza 2).

Even the vegetative world need not be motionless; for example, the trees in Eclogue 1 sway to and fro in the gentle wind. And in Eclogues 2 and 4 the activities of Flora, Natura, and Primavera, personified forces of the natural world, appear to give life to the landscape as they go about 'bordando' and 'texiendo.' There is, then, in the eclogues a constant sense of vitality and creativity, which looks to the animated world of the baroque rather than to the static creations of earlier writers, such as Garcilaso.

Baroque elements occur too in the contrasts that appear in the natural world. From mountain top we sweep rapidly to sea-level (or vice versa) more abruptly than in the gradual changes of perspective that occur, for example, in Figueroa's *Canción* 'Cantar quiero el llorar enamorado / de Beliso' or in the eclogues of Montemayor or Pedro Laynez. These sudden changes of perspective also differ from those of Herrera in that they are purely descriptive and are not intended to mirror emotions. Like the baroque artist, Torre shows a predilection for the interchanging of panoramic visions with scenes of a secluded refuge. Thus, in Eclogue 4 we move from a general scene (stanza 1) to the 'concabidades de vna piedra' (stanza 2); in Eclogue 8, from the 'amenos campos' (stanza 1) to a 'cueua vmbrosa' (stanza 8). In Eclogues 5 and 7 the process is reversed. In the former we proceed from the 'lugar' (stanza 1) to the 'florecidos campos' (stanza 3); in the latter, from the 'caberna vmbrosa' (stanza 1) to the general picture of the heavens and distant mountains (stanza 2). Eclogue 1 offers a little more variety. In stanzas 1 and 2, the poet presents the solitary Palemón. Attention then moves from the shepherd to the river bank, and rests finally on the forest (stanzas 4, 5, and 6). Suddenly, in stanza 7 the poet focuses on the nightingale, a lonely, diminutive figure perched on the branch of one of the trees. In stanza 8 we are transported equally abruptly back to a general view, that of the 'prados,' 'valles,' and 'árboles.' And, underlining all these changes, there are the rapid transformation of darkness into light and colour, the interplay of movement and repose, and the delicate balance between noise and silence.

The final impression is of a landscape that is not only more dense and colourful than that portrayed by Garcilaso and his contemporaries, but also of one that contains a greater variety of features: harmony and violence, scorching heat and the coolness of an aqueous environment, movement and noise, as well as tranquillity and silence.

Zamora Vicente makes the point of comparing Torre's descriptions with the paintings of Raphael and Titian, emphasizing the light and harmony of the compositions.[21] As a contrast to the 'sonoroso y manso Tajo' of Arcadian memory, he calls attention to the rapid movement of the river at the beginning of Góngora's 'Soledad segunda,' which he associates with the paintings of Rubens. Zamora's choice of the river comparison is rather ironic, because fast-moving rivers are one of the salient features of Torre's landscapes. Perhaps a better artistic comparison would have been between the paintings of Giorgione, whose *Fête Champêtre* (also attributed to Titian!) is surely one of the most representative of the Arcadian mood, and those of Claude Lorrain (or even Nicolas Poussin) whose canvases convey the more dynamic spirit of seventeenth-century landscapes. The Arcadian origins are still perceptible in Torre's poetry but, just as Claude has moved away from Giorgione, so too has Torre departed from the restrictions of Garcilaso's *locus amoenus*. It is no longer sufficient to characterize Torre's verse, and his landscape descriptions in particular, in the same general terms applied to Garcilaso. The songs of the shepherds are still important, but the framework in which they are set has also become an object of interest in its own right.

3

Style

Students of Spanish Golden Age literature are accustomed to reading that the verse of this period follows a trajectory that begins with Garcilaso and ends with Góngora. The former is noted for his clarity and elegance of expression; the latter is considered the most obscure of all Spanish poets. Garcilaso's poems are the epitome of simplicity; Góngora's works, especially the *Polifemo* and *Soledades*, are characterized by complex syntactic structures (with a prolific use of hyperbaton), complicated metaphors, Latinisms, and a wealth of mythological allusions. Bridging the gap between these two figures is Fernando de Herrera who, while expressing admiration for Garcilaso, sought to enrich the Spanish language and advocated innovations that prefigure the complexities of *culteranismo*.

Francisco de la Torre's poetry was seen by Quevedo, Vander Hammen, and others as an example of elegant writing unencumbered by stylistic convolutions. Certainly, when compared with the recondite imagery and inordinately complicated syntax of *culteranismo*, the verse of Francisco de la Torre does appear disarmingly simple. That simplicity, however, should be measured against the excesses that contemporary critics considered prevalent in their time and the stylistic practices of the poets of the preceding century. Dámaso Alonso was correct when he concluded, with reference to Quintana's evaluation: 'eso de la "sencillez" es mucho más complicado de lo que podrían imaginar el siglo XVIII y el XIX.'[1]

'BIMEMBRES' AND RELATED STRUCTURAL DEVICES

One aspect of Torre's language that constitutes a notable accomplishment in the stylistic trajectory between Garcilaso and Góngora is his masterly use of the *bimembre* and structural parallelism.

Of the two devices, the *bimembre* (the division of a line of poetry, especially the hendecasyllable, into two balancing parts) has received most attention. Its use by Góngora, and the analyses of this poet's work by critics (especially Dámaso Alonso), have made it a byword of seventeenth-century poetic language. It must be recognized, however, that the distinction between *bimembres* and parallelism is, at times, scarcely perceptible. Pabst, for instance, has commented that 'Con la bifurcación se obtiene la mayoría de las veces un paralelismo.'[2] Examples are not difficult to find in Torre's work:

Huyen las nubes, resplandece el cielo
      a b / a b   (Eclogue 5, stanza 18)

  rota la nieue y desligado el yelo
      a b / a b   (Sonnet 12/II)

By the same token two or more structurally parallel lines may constitute a form of prolonged *bimembre*. Dámaso Alonso has commented that 'La tendencia bilateral puede plasmar en unidades más amplias: en el conjunto de dos versos; dentro de una estrofa; entre la primera y la segunda mitad de una estrofa misma; en el conjunto de dos estrofas, etc.'[3] Again Torre provides an illuminating example:

Ya que me desespera mi ventura,
mi mucho mal, mi poco sufrimiento,
de la incierta esperança de mi vida, /
ya que me desengaña mi tormento,
mi mucho amor, mi mucha desventura
de la promesa de mi bien perdida.   (Eclogue 7, stanza 4)

It is no exaggeration to say that Spanish poets of the sixteenth century, certainly the major ones, were parsimonious users of *bimembres* and structural parallelism (although Juan de Mena, in the preceding century, was quite familiar with the technique of bifurcation).[4] For Torre, on the other hand, these devices form an integral part of his poetic language. Nevertheless, Dámaso Alonso is the only critic to have perceived Torre's use of the *bimembre* (none has commented on the parallelism!), and even he limits himself to a general observation. After discussing the infrequency of *bimembres* in the verse of Cetina and Herrera, he concludes: 'Otros poetas del siglo XVI, de los más italianizados, Francisco de la Torre, Francisco de Figueroa, por ejemplo, usaron quizá el bimembre algo más, o con más frecuente intención estética.'⁵ My reading indicates that Torre employs *bimembres* more consistently and more artistically than Figueroa or, indeed, than any other poet preceding Góngora.⁶

Torre's most skilful use of the *bimembre* is to be found in Eclogues 1 and 5, written in *octavas rimas*. Of the eight eclogues composed by him, Eclogues 1 and 5 contain significantly more *bimembres* than the other six combined (five of which are written in the *canción* combination of lines of seven and eleven syllables, and one – Eclogue 3 – in blank verse).⁷ Outside the eclogues, we also find frequent use of *bimembres* in the sonnets; their presence in the odes and *canciones*, however, is much less noticeable, owing largely to the frequency of the heptasyllables in the *canciones* and to the brevity of the strophes in the odes. The same tendency is evident in the recurrence of structural parallelism; it is frequent in the eclogues, less so in the sonnets, and rare in the other verse forms.

Rather than enumerate the examples of *bimembres* and parallelistic lines in Torre's verse, I have selected a passage in which the poet demonstrates remarkable mastery and combination of both devices, namely, the background description to Eclogue 1. In this passage Torre exhibits genuine poetic capacity in the stylistic control of a landscape that both mirrors and contrasts with the sentiments of the protagonist, Palemón. The shepherd appears on the banks of the Tagus, which is bordered by beautiful flowers and trees. In one of the trees, a nightingale gives vent to its sorrow. Beginning with stanza 4, we read:

> [El claro Tajo] Cuyas riberas claras coronadas
> de blancas flores, de purpúreas rosas,
> de plantas ameníssimas cercadas,
> quales muy raras, quales muy copiosas,
> vnas suben al cielo leuantadas,
> otras caen en las aguas sonorosas,
> haziendo todas con sus sombras bellas
> vmbrosos valles en el claro dellas.

In the first four lines of this strophe we observe the river banks crowned with white and red flowers and enclosed by 'plantas ameníssimas' (which from the following lines are evidently trees), some few in number, others in abundance. It is a most pleasant scene, the harmony of which is accentuated by the *bimembres* in the second and fourth lines, where the second part of each line structurally parallels and balances the first part. Line 2 is composed of preposition, adjective, noun/preposition, adjective, noun; line 4 consists of pronoun, adverb, adjective/pronoun, adverb, adjective. Balance and order, then, are imposed on diverse elements of nature by means of the structure of the line. There is, also, a visual balance resulting from the contrast in line 2 between white and red flowers, and in line 4 between trees few in number and trees in abundance. But the impression of balance and concord does not end at line 4. It is true that there are no further *bimembres* in this stanza, but careful reading will determine that the second half of the strophe is not without a balanced structure. Lines 5 and 6 continue the image of the trees, some reaching upward to the sky, others leaning downward towards the gently flowing water. Visually the equilibrium is evident in the contrasting motion of the trees, but structurally also the two lines mirror the balance created by the image and underline the harmony found in nature, even though the final adjectives do not modify corresponding nouns in each line. We have a parallelism of pronoun, verb, preposition, article, noun, and adjective that constitutes, within the context, a prolonged *bimembre*. The final two lines, although they depart from the bipartite character of the previous lines, preserve the established mood. This is achieved principally through enjambement (*suave*, to use Dámaso Alonso's term), which assists in reducing any impression of extreme contrast that may have been created by the rapid change of visual perspective in lines 5 and 6, and which helps to evoke a locale conducive to melancholy cogitation.

In stanza 5, the poet focuses on the elm tree, entwined on one side with the ivy and embraced on the other by the vine:

> Sube la yedra con el olmo asida
> y en otra parte con la vid ligado;
> ellas reciben de su arrimo vida
> y él de sus hojas ornamento amado;
> cuya bella corona sacudida
> mansamente del ayre regalado,
> ya se mira en el agua, y se retira,
> y luego buelue, y otra vez se mira.

The opening two lines portray principally a visual balance between the ivy and the vine, although we should not overlook the structural balance established between the two climbing plants. The ivy appears in the fourth-syllable stress position and is balanced perfectly by the vine in the eighth-syllable stress position of the following line. The balance continues in lines 3 and 4. A structural parallelism may be dimly perceived but the equilibrium is primarily conceptual, the emphasis being on confirmation of the mutual dependence of the climbing plants, which seek support, and the elm, which seeks adornment.

The second half of the strophe describes the swaying of the elm towards the water. The polysyllabic words 'corona,' 'sacudida,' 'mansamente,' and 'regalado' underline the impression of harmony, where no movement is so abrupt as to rupture the symmetry of the whole. The final two lines complete the image of the swaying of the tree with a magnificence that even Garcilaso might envy. Line 7 depicts the first half of the movement as the elm leans over the water and then gently withdraws ('ya se mira en el agua, y se retira'). The verbs significantly are situated in initial and final positions, whereby they not only control the motion of the tree but also structurally underline the first half of the movement. Line 8 portrays the complementary half-movement whereby the elm returns to its original position. Again the structure reflects the continuity of movement, unhurried and harmonious as the swaying of a tree should be. The continuity is conveyed by a judicious repetition of the conjunction 'y,' which unites the two halves of the *bimembre*, by the parallel balance of the two adverbs 'luego' and 'otra vez,' and by the artistic use of epanalepsis, or the repetition of a word beginning a line at the end of either that or the following line. The verb 'se mira' not only returns us both structurally and visually to the beginning of line 7 and to the onset of the movement, but also suggests excellently the commencement of yet another circular motion.

Stanza 5 ends with a *bimembre*; the first half of stanza 6 continues and intensifies the use of the device:

> El verde mirto y el laurel hermoso,
> aquél a Venus, éste a Febo caro;
> el derecho ciprés y álamo vmbroso,
> aquél oscuro y éste verde claro;
> el plátano y el cedro, y oloroso
> sobre todos gentil líbano raro,
> su lugar apacible coronando,
> aquí y allí los tray el ayre blando.

If we consider the first two lines (a couplet), we will observe that line 1 contains two objects, 'mirto' (A) and 'laurel' (B). Line 2 introduces two figures, 'Venus' (A'), who corresponds to the myrtle, and 'Febo' (B'), corresponding to the laurel. The following couplet, lines 3 and 4, is constructed in parallel fashion: 'ciprés' (C) modified by 'oscuro' (C'), and 'álamo' (D) modified by 'verde claro' (D'). The first four lines, then, consist of a series of nouns, pronouns, and adjectives, which in effect constitutes enumeration. One of the effects of enumeration, as indicated by Kayser, is the loss of identity or individual characteristics of objects.[8] To this I would add the possible creation of a lack of order or control. None of these effects, however, occurs in the present strophe. The trees maintain their identity and order and symmetry are preserved, thanks to the bipartite structure of the lines. The reader's imagination is simply prohibited from moving in unrestrained fashion.

Not only is each individual line of the first half of stanza 6 a *bimembre* but line 1 may also be considered to form the first half of a larger *bimembre*, the second half of which is line 2. Lines 3 and 4 are structured in parallel manner. But we can now go one step further and consider that lines 1 and 2 together form the first half of an even larger *bimembre*, the second half being completed by lines 3 and 4. The whole structure of these four lines, then, is based entirely on parallel complementaries, each constantly balancing the other and thus controlling the effusive, unrestrained effect that enumeration may have. Graphically, the structure may be represented as follows:

$$
\left.\begin{array}{l}
\text{line 1: A / B} \\
\text{line 2: A'/ B'}
\end{array}\right\}
\left.\begin{array}{l}
\text{A + B / A' + B'} \\
\\
\text{C + D / C' + D'}
\end{array}\right\}
\text{A + B, A' + B'/ C + D, C' + D'}
$$
$$
\left.\begin{array}{l}
\text{line 3: C / D} \\
\text{line 4: C'/ D'}
\end{array}\right\}
$$

In contrast to the first four lines, the stanza's second four lines contain no structural devices that impose control. Nevertheless, the impression of restraint evoked in the first half is maintained by the enjambement *suave*, the bipartite nature of the two adverbs 'aquí' and 'allí,' and by the adjectives 'gentil,' 'apacible,' and 'blando.'

The lack of rigid structural control in the second half of stanza 6 directs us stylistically towards stanza 7, in which there is a noticeable absence of *bimembres* or parallelism:

Entre cuyas vmbrosas ramas bellas,
Filomena dulcíssima cantando
ensordece la selua con querellas,
su grauíssimo daño lamentando;
lleuan los ayres los acentos dellas
los montes y las cueuas resonando,
de donde, con tristíssimo gemido,
eco responde al canto dolorido.

The departure in this strophe from the stylistic procedure of stanzas 4, 5, and 6 is significant because the theme also differs. No longer is there a presentation of a beautiful, serene world, where the emphasis is on harmony and reciprocal movement. The focus is now upon the philomel, or nightingale, traditionally a symbol of sorrow. Accordingly the vocabulary reflects this shift in emphasis, there being a preponderance of words conveying sorrow ('querellas,' 'grauíssimo daño lamentando,' 'tristíssimo gemido,' 'canto dolorido'). Where *bimembres* and parallelism earlier had underlined the harmony of the natural world, their absence here accentuates the sorrow of the bird and its inability to participate in the surrounding harmony. This effect is heightened, furthermore, by the fact that the bird, an integral part of the natural world, is seated in the very trees that were employed to convey harmony.

The thematic and structural deviation of stanza 7 is further emphasized by the return, in stanza 8, to the subject and arrangement of the earlier strophes:

Donde mirando los alegres prados,
valles vmbrosos y árboles floridos,
de blancas, rojas flores matizados,
vnos brotando y otros florecidos,
los dorados cristales sossegados,
los animosos vientos desparcidos,
la Primauera con la bella Flora
que vna los viste y otra los colora.

The first three lines, containing a certain degree of enumeration, recall the second half of stanza 6 by their lack of rigid, structural control. Furthermore, they mirror the situation of Palemón who, like the nightingale, is a part of the natural world, and like her is unable to participate in the harmony he views around him. Nevertheless, it will be noted that, as our attention moves away from Palemón and the nightingale and back to the landscape, the structural aspect of the stanza becomes more stylized and controlled with the reappearance of *bimembres* and parallelism. The first example of *bimembre* occurs in line 4 ('vnos brotando y otros florecidos'). While the line may not constitute a grammatically perfect balance ('brotando' being a gerund and 'florecidos' a past participle), the interplay of 'vnos' and 'otros' clearly announces its bipartite character. Stylistically, line 4 reduces any acceleration that enumeration ('prados,' 'valles,' 'árboles,' 'blancas, rojas flores') may cause, balances the duality of 'blancas' and 'rojas,' and forecasts the more rigid control of the second half of the strophe.

Lines 5 and 6 of stanza 8 present simultaneously structural parallelism and visual contrast and balance. The structural parallelism is easily observed: definite article, adjective, noun, past participle (with adjectival function) in both lines. The visual contrast and balance may be perceived in the duality of water and wind, the water calm and golden-coloured at ground level, the wind fast-moving and scattered throughout the heavens. The duality is continued in the bipartite nature of line 7 (there is no structural balance, but a certain equilibrium is imposed by the initial position of 'Primauera' and the final placement of 'Flora') and underlined by the concluding line of the strophe, structurally a *bimembre*. The function of this particular *bimembre*, unlike that of line 4 (curbing the impression of acceleration), is to complete the bipartite nature of the second half of the stanza and to perfect visually the harmonious activities of 'Primauera' and 'Flora.'

The *bimembre* is a fitting stylistic means of concluding the landscape description of Eclogue 1, one that leaves the reader with an impression of order and concord. The landscape appears to form a rhythmic pattern that is ruptured only by the plaintive song of the nightingale. Such a pattern is underlined by the presence of the stylistic devices used, and the schism symbolized by their absence.

The description of the landscape demonstrates that *bimembres* and parallelism were not artifices haphazardly employed by Torre but were consciously introduced by a poet well aware of the artistic potential of the technique of bifurcation. The control created by the devices need be not only visual (as in the passage discussed) but also emotional, as stanza 9 of the same eclogue indicates:

Y que el rigor de su dolor esquiuo,
que la dureza de su ninfa bella,
que la firmeza que le tiene viuo
crece, ni mengua su fatal estrella,
de su crueldad, de su desdén altiuo,
tan tierna y tristemente se querella,
que el monte ablanda, que detiene el río,
el cielo pára, inclina el viento frío.

The anaphora of the first three lines creates a certain tension as the reader awaits the principal clause, but the nature of the tension is subdued with a note of resignation. This is due to not only the bent of Palemón's complaint ('tan tierna ... se querella') but also the parallelism of the first two lines (the third only varies slightly) and, in particular, to the *bimembres* of the final two lines. Here the balancing parallelism (line 7, a b / b a; line 8 a b / b a) corresponds perfectly to the decreased activity of mountain, river, sky, and wind. At the same time it reduces significantly the feeling of anger evoked by such words as 'rigor,' 'dureza,' 'firmeza,' 'crueldad,' 'fatal estrella,' and 'desdén,' and imposes thereby a kind of emotional symmetry and control. It is a technique that suggests restraint on the emotions and a certain aloofness, and may help to justify Dámaso Alonso's assertion that Torre is a 'cold' poet.[9]

The technique of bifurcation is one for which Góngora is widely renowned. Nevertheless, from the examination of the foregoing strophes, it may be argued that Torre displays a mastery of the *bimembre* and parallelism that few, if any, poets of the Golden Age (other than Góngora) surpass.[10] *Bimembres* and parallelism were not unknown to earlier sixteenth-century Spanish poets but were used most infrequently in their verse. What makes the devices more 'baroque' in Torre's work is their intensified use and, as the poet demonstrates, their potentially complex combinations.

As indicated in note 6, *bimembres* and parallelism are not the only structural tools that attracted Torre's attention. The repetitive use of epanalepsis is remarkable, and more frequent than suggested by Dámaso Alonso in his article.[11] Nevertheless, it corresponds perfectly with Torre's predilection for balanced symmetrical structural devices and provides a certain architectural quality to his verse.

The effect of epanalepsis varies according to the context, but the general tendency is to recall artistically and thereby emphasize rhythmically a point or mood that the poet wishes to evoke:

crece mi miedo y mi tormento crece   (Sonnet 27/1)

llorando me dejas,
hállasme llorando   (Endecha 9)

Solo por la ribera sola llega,
de su dolor acompañado solo   (Eclogue 1, stanza 3)

The device may be no more than reversed parallelism:

Desengañado de mi bien agora,
agora de mi bien desengañado[12]   (Eclogue 7, stanza 6)

A contrast in fortune may be effectively conveyed:

Tú fuiste querida,
y oluidada fuiste.   (Endecha 6)

ha sido llorado,
y aliuiado ha sido   (Endecha 9)

An extended example can help prolong emotion, as in the sorrow of a shepherdess:

Y auiendo con svspiros dolorosos,
con tristíssimas lágrimas auiendo
su gravíssima pena declarado,
deteniendo los vientos animosos,
las sonoras aguas deteniendo
con vn boluer de ojos sossegado.   (Eclogue 4, stanza 12)

As seen earlier, the gentle swaying and circular motion of a tree is brilliantly evoked:

Ya se mira en el agua y se retira
y luego buelue, y otra vez se mira   (Eclogue 1, stanza 5)

In the following example the repetition enhances the atmosphere of evening calm and reflects structurally the image conveyed by 'cerco':

Serénase la noche, y el turbado
cerco del ancho seno se serena.   (Eclogue 7, stanza 3)

A similar use of epanalepsis in the final lines of Eclogue 3 conveys excellently the mood of resignation of the shepherd as he terminates his song:

paze el ganado mustio y él al río,
y él al pasto, y al monte se va solo;
solo se va buscando sus vezerros,
y a la cabaña sola se va solo.

Here the notion of solitude, vaguely reminiscent of stanza 34 of San Juan de la Cruz's 'Cántico espiritual,' recalls the isolation to which the shepherd draws attention at the beginning of his lament ('En tanto yo ... / conmigo solo cantaré mi pena,' 11.10–12). The emphatic reiteration of not only 'solo' but also the verb 'se va' is the climax of the poem and embraces, as it were, the whole eclogue in a mood of melancholy isolation.

There is no doubt that the frequent use of epanalepsis by Torre demonstrates a conscious effort at rhetorical artifice. In addition, there are numerous instances where the repetition is not perfect, but a similarity of verb tense, a variant of a word, and contrast justify inclusion here and serve to underline the fascination of the device for Torre. The following are but a few examples of modified epanalepsis:

Suspiro de contino y suspirando	(Sonnet 2/II)
Dorando el Norte y el Ocaso hiriendo	(Canción 3/II)
Lléuame la tormenta en el momento por donde viuiente no lleuara	(Sonnet 19/II)
Tú quieres matarme, darte vida quiero	(Endecha 4)
Llegó mi lamentable pena donde mi desuentura miserable llega	(Eclogue 7, stanza 5)

Isolated instances of epanalepsis may be found in works of other sixteenth-century poets, but none employed it so studiously as Francisco de la Torre.[13] And yet, unlike *bimembres*, it is a mannerism that did not appear to enjoy much success with later poets either. The reason for its popularity with Torre is most likely to be found in his close acquaintance with classical poets, especially Horace, and in the fact that it probably represented one of the ways in which he sought to give his verse a classical flavour, in keeping with the fashion of the latter half of the sixteenth century.[14]

An echo of Torre's predilection for structural balance is to be found also in the reiteration of words in the middle of a line (a device akin to chiasmus). Examples are not many, but even so their number exceeds the use by other poets of the sixteenth century. We have the following:

Vuelas al fin y al fin te vas llorando	(Canción 1/I)
Corona clara y clara Casiopea	(Ode 5/II)
En paz te queda, queda en paz amada	(Eclogue 2, stanza 14)
Injusto amor, amor injusto y fiero	(Eclogue 6, stanza 24)

Y quanto me huye más, más me enamora   (Sonnet 10/II)

Muere por Daphnis, Daphnis inhumana   (Eclogue 5, stanza 27)

The care with which Torre artistically uses *bimembres*, parallelism, and epanalepsis suggests an equally assiduous attention to other structural devices. The *trimembre*, for one, is certainly a part of his technique, as noted by Agustín del Campo and Dámas Alonso, but its success is less evident than that of the *bimembre*.[15] Nevertheless, one variant – the use of the same word three times in the same line – is of some interest:

Inclina el sol, inclina el cielo, inclina / los elementos   (Sonnet 2/I)

de verdes hojas, verde vid y verde / yedra   (Canción 1/I)

bella si cruda, bella esquiua y bella   (Sonnet 23/I)

admira el cielo, admira el mundo, admira / la causa   (Eclogue 1, stanza 14)

Of course these examples constitute, in effect, epanalepsis with great emphasis being conveyed by not simply the repetition but also the strong rhythmic stress-location of the repeated words. Apart from these quotations, however, there is nothing to distinguish Torre from other sixteenth-century practitioners of the *trimembre*.

Torre does not appear to surpass his contemporaries, either, in the use of correlation. His admittedly few attempts belong, in Dámaso Alonso's words, to 'Los tipos de correlación menos extravagantes.'[16] Indeed one might go further than Alonso (who elsewhere states that Torre uses correlation 'en su forma genuina')[17] and argue that correlation was a device that he did not master completely. Its principal function, that of verbal compression, is never achieved with the perfection of Herrera or of later writers, such as Góngora, Quevedo, or Calderón. Nowhere, for instance, in Torre's verse does the line containing the correlative sequence follow the order in which the sequence is presented. This is so even in Sonnet 7/II, which owes so much to Benedetto Varchi's sonnet, 'Questo è, Tirsi, quel fonte in cui solea.'[18] In the latter the sequence is arranged: 'fonte' (1), 'prati' (2), 'elce' (3), 'antro' (4). The correlating line is 'All'antro [4], dunque all'elce [3], ai prati [2], al fonte [1].' It is true that the order has been reversed, but there is at least uniformity. In Torre's poem the first sequence is arranged: 'fuente' (1), 'prado' (2), 'haya' (3), 'cueua' (4), 'monte' (5); and the correlating line is 'Al prado [2], y haya [3], y cueua [4] y monte [5], y fuente [1].' The absence of complete consistency is certainly not extreme, but it does reflect a weakness that Torre never overcomes.[19]

The lack of marked poetic skill in the use of correlation or even *trimembres* should not blind us to the remarkable originality and artistry that Torre displays in his handling of *bimembres* and parallelism. It is not so much the recurrent presence of these devices that startles as the effect with which Torre employed them. Epanalepsis, too, mirrors an ever-increasing artificiality of syntax, although it did not develop into a major poetic tool of seventeenth-century poets. It presents no syntactic difficulty for the reader, but nonetheless could be very effectively used in the hands of such a practised poet as Francisco de la Torre.

SYNTAX

Hyperbaton

In view of the deliberate and controlled effect of the structural devices discussed above, it is not surprising that Torre should not be a great exponent of hyperbaton, the inversion of normal word order. Naturally, the artificial placing of words that epanalepsis implies does frequently suggest a degree of syntactic inversion, but poetic language itself often involves some transposition of word order. Certainly the kind of hyperbaton that Torre employs is not difficult and can be found in the verse of any Spanish poet of the sixteenth century. The conspicuous absence of this 'vice' of *culteranismo* in Torre's poetry was undoubtedly an important consideration in the praise of both Quevedo and Vander Hammen.

Subordinate Clauses

At the same time, however, it should not be assumed that Torre's verse is entirely characterized by symmetry and structural control. On the contrary, there is another side to his style, best exemplified – like the use of *bimembres* and parallelism – in the eclogues. However, whereas *bimembres* and parallelism prevail in Eclogues 1 and 5, both composed in *octavas rimas*, the 'other side' is prominent in Eclogues 2, 4, 6, and 8, written in *estancias* (strophes consisting of a combination of hendecasyllables and heptasyllables).

The outstanding syntactic feature in Eclogues 2, 4, 6, and 8 is the recurrent interpolation of subordinate clauses in the background descriptions. Indeed the large number of subordinate clauses makes it often difficult to determine the principal clause at the beginning of these poems. The first strophe of Eclogue 4, for example, describes the arrival of spring and the rebirth of beauty and colour. The lack of a main verb, together with the repeated use of gerunds ('coronando,' 'bordando,' 'vistiendo,' 'entretexiendo'), gives rise to an ever-increasing and seemingly endless accumulation of natural wealth. The second stanza changes initially from the temporal framework of stanza 1 ('Al tiempo que ...') to the physical ('en las concabidades de vna piedra') before returning, in line 10, to the temporal ('Al tiempo que ...'). The situation is not clarified in stanza 3; we can only feel that something is to happen at a certain place, as suggested by 'en las concabidades' (stanza 2) and 'aquí' (stanza 3), and at a certain time, in the evening. The series of verbs in stanza 3 ('resonaua,' 'se metía,' 'resonauan,' 'suspendía,' and 'meneaua') have no true verbal function but add to the impression of accumulation like the gerunds in the first stanza. The beginning of stanza 4 again affirms the time of day – evening (described in mythological terms) – before we are finally informed of the presence of a certain forlorn shepherd, Tirsis. Attention is now focused on the shepherd, but still there is no main clause. Finally, in stanza 5, we learn that Tirsis 'tales estremos suspirando hazía,' and that 'los peñascos duros ablandara / si consistiera en ellos el sentido / que en su ninfa terrible consistía, / Filis, sin duda su enemiga cara.' But this is not the end. By his use of 'cuya' the poet appends further information – this time about the effects of Filis's beauty – before concluding with a return to Tirsis: 'quando, cobrando su perdido aliento, / assí soltó la triste voz al viento.'

The effect of the five strophes is one of increasing disorientation as the reader awaits the principal clause – promised in line 1 of stanza 1, again in lines 1 and 10 of stanza 2, again in lines 1 of stanzas 3 and 4 – which appears finally in stanza 5. And even here the main clause is not clearly identifiable. Is it 'Tirsis cuytado ... / tales estremos suspirando hazía,' or 'Tirsis cuytado ... / assí soltó la voz al viento'?

The effect is, as I have remarked, one of disorientation, but there is also an intellectual demand made on the reader to strive to separate and keep the information in perspective. In the description there is an unrestrained exuberance that differs quite radically from the impression conveyed by the description of the landscape background of Eclogue 1. In the first eclogue there is much exuberance and profusion but, owing to the stylistic devices employed, there is always control and symmetry. Such controlling devices, with the exception of the *bimembre* in the final line of stanza 1, are conspicuously absent in Eclogue 4. In particular, the repeated use of gerunds in the first strophe results in an acute impression of accumulation: we scarcely see the flowers on the river banks before being deluged by the 'viuos colores' spread over the fields, and by the green leaves of trees and the red petals of flowers.

A similar procedure to that seen in Eclogue 4 may also be perceived in Eclogue 2, although the background description itself is shorter, consisting of only three stanzas. The repeated use of gerunds and the general absence of controlling structural devices evoke an impression of exuberance, as Flora and Natura – personified natural forces – scatter colour and warmth about the river banks. The first two stanzas focus on this pre-nocturnal activity while stanza 3 specifies the approach of night ('Al tiempo que ...,' again in mythological terms), before finally introducing the protagonist, the forlorn Tirsis.

In Eclogue 8 the principal clause appears in stanza 2, where we are informed that 'El ausente pastor Montano vino / a la frescura de vna cueua vmbrosa.' The introduction of the main clause in the second strophe is relatively early in comparison with its appearance in Eclogues 2, 4, and 6, but Torre's familiar techniques, beginning with the temporal framework 'Al tiempo que ...' (stanza 1, line 1), are not overlooked. Following the reference to Montano, Torre returns to the interpolated clauses – here accentuated by the possessive relative 'cuyo' – with no syntactic respite until Montano's lament begins in stanza 7.

In Eclogue 6, the background description is not one of peace and profusion, but stylistically we are confronted with the same procedure noted for Eclogues 4, 2 and 8. Stanza 1 portrays the place ('En vna yertas rocas rigurosas'); stanza 2 depicts a storm and its effects; stanza 3 informs us that there is a person lamenting his misfortune; and stanza 4, which provides the temporal framework, finally reveals the identity of Florelo.

We can, perhaps, best measure the degree of complexity in the eclogues discussed if we consider the number of subordinate clauses that occur between the initial statement and the principal clauses (I include, too, the gerunds because of their accumulative effect). In Eclogue 4 we find (if we accept 'assí soltó la triste voz al viento' as the main clause) twenty-three subordinate verbs and eight gerunds; in Eclogue 2, sixteen subordinate verbs and twelve gerunds; in Eclogue 8, four secondary clauses and two gerunds preceding the main verb, the ratio increasing in the remainder of the description to twenty-three to four; and, finally, in Eclogue 6, eighteen subordinate verbs and five gerunds. The total in each eclogue is quite startling, and perhaps unexpected in a poet who could so successfully show structural control. And yet the repeated practice of accumulation was surely no more haphazard than the symmetry of the background description of Eclogue 1. Despite the objections of Mariano José Quintana that 'A veces ... la locución se manifiesta oscura por dislocaciones u omisiones de expresiones, acaso hijas del descuido y corrupción de los manuscritos'[20] – which could well have the opening stanzas of Eclogues 2, 4, 6, and 8 in mind – it does appear unusual that a poet should be 'careless' in so many instances. The logical sequence of the rhyme scheme also suggests that the manuscripts were not incomplete. It seems, rather, that accumulation of subordinate clauses is another characteristic (perhaps weakness) of Torre's style that other poets of the sixteenth century do not appear to have shared. Its use exclusively in the background descriptions of the eclogues may have been provoked by a desire to capture the variety and seeming endless configurations of nature in a manner vaguely reminiscent of Góngora's *Soledades*. But it is equally likely that it was inspired by Torre's wish to imitate the complexity of Latin compositions. In any case, it undoubtedly anticipates the intricacies of *culteranismo*. Some remarks by two writers on Góngora's verse might well apply to the landscape descriptions in the above eclogues: in the opinion of María Rosa Lida de Malkiel, the *Soledades* contain 'Serpenteo de ... aposiciones, ... intercalares ... disjuntivas, ... relativos';[21] and Dámaso Alonso talks of the 'empleo singular de los relativos, complicación y longitud del período gramatical, lleno de incisos de valor diferente, de paréntesis enteramente desligados, de aposiciones, de gerundios ...'[22]

Gerunds

Alonso's passing remark about the gerund in connection with Góngora is a reminder that the principal exponent of *culteranismo* has a worthy forerunner in Torre. Certainly, like the past participle, the gerund by the very nature of its ending lends itself well to the rhyme scheme of a poem, and Torre, like other poets, did not hesitate to make use of it. Sometimes the poetic impact is minimal, but on other occasions the device is employed with considerable artistic flair. In the first stanzas of Eclogues 2 and 4 respectively (mentioned above), the activities of Flora, Natura, and Primauera are particularly enhanced by the undulating and continuous movement suggested by such gerunds as 'bordando,' 'texiendo,' 'clarificando,' and 'vistiendo.' In Eclogue 5, stanza 17, attention is drawn to the arrival of Aurora by a series of gerunds, all appearing at the end of their respective lines:

Blancas, purpúreas flores produziendo,
prados, valles, montes aljofarando,
las sombras de la noche deshaziendo,
los ayres y los cielos alegrando,
rompió la Aurora con su luz, saliendo.

The effect is striking: after the darkness of night and the lament of Palemón – in which the gerund rarely occurs – the harmony and beauty that accompany the dawn are mirrored effectively by the intensified use of the device, with its marked rhythmic quality. And the repeated '-ndo' sound in identical position facilitates the rhyme scheme; at the same time it serves as a unifying element among the various objects of the world (flowers, meadows, valleys, mountains, breezes, and the sky) and is a constant factor that links them with Aurora. A final effect is that of a heightened sense of anticipation as the reader awaits the main information to be divulged by the principal clause.

It would be unwise to overemphasize the role of the gerund in his verse, but the manner in which Torre uses it suggests that he was not unaware of its poetic impact. The procedure followed in stanza 17 of Eclogue 5 is imitated in identical manner in stanza 22, where the arrival of several nymphs is seen to have profound effects upon the earth and the heavens. In stanza 30 of the same eclogue the reverse pattern is used – the main clause precedes the series of gerunds, – but the purpose remains much the same. Other examples of the gerund in a prominent role are to be found in Ode 2/I, stanzas 5, 6, and 7; Ode 1/II stanzas 3 and 4; and Eclogue 6, stanzas 19 and 20.

Cuyo

The accumulative effect that interpolated subordinate clauses and a series of gerunds can have is well illustrated by yet another poetic device much favoured by Torre, one little used by other Spanish poets of the sixteenth century: the possessive relative pronoun 'cuyo.' It is not only the frequency of 'cuyo' in Torre's verse (in the eclogues alone it appears forty-one times compared to ten in all of Garcilaso's poetry) that is of interest, but also the manner in which it is employed. The normal position of the relative is that immediately following the noun (or pronoun) that is its antecedent, and there are numerous such instances in Torre's verse. However, Torre frequently, and in a manner highly disconcerting to the modern reader, also introduces the possessive relative at the beginning of a clause or 'sentence' precisely when a syntactic or conceptual respite is anticipated. Stanzas 19, 20, and 21 of Eclogue 4 offer good examples:

(Stanza 19)
    Poco a poco se fueron recogiendo [Tirsis and la ninfa]
    a la parte del valle más sombría.
    Cuya caberna vmbría,
    de plantas coronada,
    de flores matizada,
    es deleytosa parte defendida.

(Stanza 20)
> De donde sobre mármoles de Paro,
> como la nieue de la sierra elada,
> vna fuente claríssima salía;
> cuyo cristal, más puro, viuo y claro
> que el agua de la sierra despeñada,
> el alameda fresca produzía.
> Donde después que auía,
> por vn camino vsado,
> los árboles regado,
> por vnos yertos riscos empinados
> del curso de las aguas quebrantados,
> haziendo vn ronco son de peña en peña,
> en el sagrado río se despeña.

(Stanza 21)
> Cuya rara belleza contemplando,
> del deleytoso valle conuidados,
> en torno de la fuente se sentaron.

In each of the above cases the possessive relative adds further information about the nouns which is syntactically unexpected and which, together with the curiously parallel use of the adverb 'donde' in stanza 20 (lines 1 and 7), directs the reader inexorably onward. And since the focus of attention in this passage is the stream issuing forth from the 'fuente claríssima,' the device is most appropriate, reinforcing the increasing movement of the water as it proceeds to the 'sagrado río.'

A careful reading of Torre's verse will reveal that the possessive relative occurs principally in the eclogues and the *canciones* (it appears in only two sonnets, 23/I and 31/II; one ode, 3/II, stanza 13; and three *endechas*, 3, 9, 10), forms that are marked by fairly long strophes and in which nature plays an important role. The impact of 'cuyo' in such poems greatly assists the impression of accumulation often desired when describing the landscape. Thus its use in the opening stanzas of Eclogue 8, alluded to earlier in connection with subordinate clauses. In Eclogue 1, stanzas 4 and 5, the focus is upon the colourful banks of the Tagus, and the elm tree embraced by the ivy and the vine; in Eclogue 5, stanzas 1 and 2, attention is directed to the rocky banks of the Tagus as the river speeds to the ocean.

In many instances, including some of those above, the possessive relative causes a certain disorientation in the reader, because it not only begins a clause but also refers back to a noun that does not immediately precede it. This technique, used once by Garcilaso in stanza 1 of his first eclogue, obliges the reader to search for the relevant noun and, in a sense, keeps him intellectually active and not a little surprised. For example, not one of the four possessive relatives of Eclogue 8, stanzas 2, 3, and 5 modifies a noun immediately preceding it. In stanza 2, 'cuya florida entrada' (line 7) refers to 'cueua' (line 5); 'De cuyo presuroso y presto curso' (stanza 3, line 1) looks back to 'cristalino Tajo' (stanza 2, line 13); 'Cuyo lugar sombrío' (stanza 5, line 7) modifies 'seluas' (stanza 5, line 6); and 'Cuyas concabidades espaciosas' (stanza 5, line 1) is separated from its noun, 'cabernas' (stanza 4, line 10), by four lines. In Eclogue 4, stanza 11, the possessive in line 1 reaches back eight lines to the 'ninfa' of stanza 10, line 6; Eclogue 1 contains an extreme example whereby the 'De cuyo grave daño lastimado' (stanza 10, line 1) in effect refers back to Palemón in stanza 1.

Abundant use of the possessive relative is an accepted characteristic of *culto* poets and imparts a Latin flavour to their verse when it is employed as the principal word of a clause.[23] The constant presence and the manner of use of 'cuyo' in Torre's verse coincide with his predilection for accumulated subordinate clauses and mark Torre as a pre-*culto* poet of more than passing interest.

Enumeration and Anaphora

In my discussion of the landscape background of Eclogue 1 (pages 61–6), I noted how *bimembres* imposed an element of control and order on the enumerated objects and prevented their loss of complete individuality. The same phenomenon may be observed in stanza 39 of the same poem, or in the description of Filis in Eclogue 5, stanza 19, or in the effects of the beloved in Sonnet 14/I. A common feature of these examples – apart from the *bimembres* – is that the stanzas are hendecasyllabic, which facilitates the creation of symmetry and the retention of the independence of the enumerated objects.

On occasion, however, the enumeration is so prolonged, or the controlling device plays so minor a role (or is even absent), that the enumerated items are converted into impressionistic images. The metaphoric and hyperbolic description of Galatea in stanza 9 of Eclogue 6 comes to mind. In Eclogue 2, stanza 5, the enumerated sequence is dominated by a succession of verbs ('detiene,' 'serena,' 'tray,' 'refrena,' 'colora,' 'suspende'), each appearing at the beginning of a line (the first form in consecutive lines) and designed to strengthen the effect of the shepherdess's presence. Yet, even within this succession of verbs, we may observe an even greater accumulation of the elements affected ('Sol,' 'viento,' 'Primauera,' 'luz,' 'Aurora,' 'día,' 'ira ...

del mar,' 'monte,' 'prado,' 'rayos'). The impression that the reader retains from this accumulation within accumulation is that Filis's presence has an immense impact upon nature. Individual consequences, however, are lost, submerged in the hyperbolic portrayal of Filis's power.

The appearance of inflected verbs at the beginning or end of lines in rapid succession is a common characteristic of Torre's verse and echoes his practice of placing gerunds in a particular sequence. The inflected verbs are especially notable in the background descriptions in Eclogues 2, 4, and 6. In Eclogue 2, stanza 3 we read that

> los vientos amansaua,
> el río detenía
> las aues suspendía
> el desdichado Tirsi.

Stanza 3 of Eclogue 4 tells us that

> aquí donde la fuente resonaua,
> el ayre entre las flores se metía,
> los valles resonauan sin aliento,
> el viento su braueza suspendía
> y las yeruas y rosas meneaua.

Finally, in Eclogue 6, stanza 2 we are informed that the north wind

> turba furiosamente su sossiego,
> deshoja y quiebra el árbol más seguro,
> ciega la vista con el presto fuego
> del centro hasta las nubes leuantado,
> abrasa el verde prado,
> altera el manso viento,
> esconde el firmamento,
> haze temblar la cumbre leuantada.

What we have in these excerpts is a sudden acceleration of accumulation within passages that contain numerous subordinate clauses. In Eclogues 2 and 6, furthermore, the increased accumulation coincides with heptasyllabic lines which, being shorter, augment the sensation of acceleration.

Unlike the structural devices or the deliberate accumulation of subordinate clauses, which we have already discussed, enumeration does not stand out so clearly as a stylistic characteristic of Torre's verse, perhaps because it lacks definable or easily recognizable features or it tends to be a part of daily life, in some form or other. Nevertheless, enumeration can have considerable artistic impact when used in certain contexts and governed by a poetic mind.

Like enumeration, repetition is a term that generally does not convey much poetic connotation nowadays. And yet epanalepsis and correlation are forms of repetition, which, when used with artistic flair, can enhance any poetic context. Anaphora is another variation of repetition and Torre resorts to it frequently, certainly more so than Garcilaso. There are instances when the impact of the anaphora is modest, but there are also more complex combinations that have a much more powerful effect. Stanzas 15 and 16 of Eclogue I, for example, come to mind:

(Stanza 15)
Nunca Iúpiter muestra su potencia
eternamente al aflixido suelo;
nunca de turbias nube [sic] la inclemencia
esconde la diuina luz del cielo;
nunca del Austro crudo la violencia
junta de nieblas espantoso velo;
nunca dura la mar alboratada,
fortuna nunca sigue tan ayrada.

(Stanza 16)
Quando persigue, quando fauorece,
quando amenaza cielo, mar y tierra,
agora paz, agora guerra ofrece,
ofrece paz, y ofrece cruda guerra;
agora de su mal se compadece
y agora hiere la empinada sierra,
arrebatando de la vista el cielo
con rayos, vientos, aguas, nieblas, yelo.

In stanza 15, the negative anaphora (reminiscent of the practice of Horace) establishes a strict pattern as the initial word in lines 1, 3, 5, and 7, and reinforces Palemón's message. This pattern is disrupted in line 8 in two ways: first, by the presence of 'nunca' in an even line, and, second, by its position as the second word in the line. The break in the order serves perhaps two functions: it averts the possible monotony that an established pattern can create; and it is a stylistic preparation for the structural irregularity of stanza 16, in a manner that echoes the earlier procedure between stanzas 6 and 7 of the same eclogue.

Stanza 16 is a remarkable combination of symmetrical devices, anaphora and enumeration, and yet there is no clear or consistent structural pattern. It again mirrors, I feel, Torre's ability to make rhetorical devices reflect the tone of a passage. Following the rhythmic anaphora of stanza 15, Torre switches in stanza 16 to a structure that promises some kind of symmetry but that in fact constantly changes. Line 1, with its *bimembre*, holds out the expectation of more symmetry to follow; the triple 'quando' together with corresponding verbs are echoed by three nouns ('cielo,' 'mar,' and 'tierra') but the balance is illusory, as the very verbs ('persigue,' 'fauorece,' and 'amenaza') and the nouns suggest. Lines 3 and 4 seem to be *bimembres* and seem to be parallel but they are not: both lines are divided into sections of four and seven syllables, and the order of the repeated words in line 4 is completely dislocated. Similarly lines 5 and 6 appear to be parallelistic (an impression strengthened by the initial 'agora' in each line), but again the appearance is deceptive. The stanza concludes with a series of five nouns that recall the five examples of fortune's characteristics outlined in stanza 15, but they do not correlate perfectly. The whole point of the stanza is that it structurally mirrors the everlasting changeability of fortune (recall the peace-war image of lines 3–4, stanza 16), which now favours the lover, now renders him disconsolate. It is clear, then, that stanza 16 is on the one hand deliberately composed of elements that suggest symmetry (and thereby the favours of fortune), but on the other hand, its very incompletion or inconsistency points to the other face of fortune. (In this respect, also, the anaphora of stanza 16 has nothing of the consistency of the 'nunca' of the preceding stanza.)

The above stanzas contain several examples of anaphora within a limited number of lines. Nevertheless, anaphora prolonged over more than one strophe was not unknown to Torre. The interrogative '¿Viste?' for instance, is the initial word of the first four stanzas of Ode 4/I. The greeting 'Salue,' addressed to dawn, occurs in three consecutive stanzas of Ode 3/I, and stanzas 4, 5, and 6 of Ode 5/II commence with the exclamatory '¡Quántas vezes!' In these examples, any tension arising from rapid repetition virtually disappears and the anaphora now serves the important role of a unifying device, reminding the reader of the poet's objective within a series of strophes. Thus, for example, the repetition of '¿Viste?' in Ode 4/I unites the disparate elements ('cierua,' 'cielo,' 'noche,' 'garza,' 'flores') listed by the poet, and consistently recalls the underlying theme of the work: the swift and sudden change of fortune.[24]

IMAGERY

Simile

In a brief discussion of Garcilaso's style, Margot Arce has commented that 'Cuantitativamente las metáforas son escasas y las comparaciones y símiles mucho más abundantes.'[25] In comparison with Garcilaso's verse, Torre's poetry is characterized by a relative paucity of similes and not a single example of the extended simile. This is quite unusual, given its constant use in the sixteenth century. And even when Torre does employ a simile it is inevitably introduced by 'como' or 'tal' or 'assí' and on only one occasion (in Eclogue 2, stanza 1) does he use 'cual,' the poetic form so frequently preferred in the second half of the sixteenth century.

Torre's preference, reminiscent of a technique practised by Cetina, is for a kind of intermediary stage between a simile and a metaphor, in which the first component of the simile (the 'como') is either delayed (Sonnet 31/II) or completely omitted (Sonnet 2/I; Ode 4/I, stanza 6; Eclogue I, stanza 31). The effect is to emphasize the comparative element by virtue of the surprise factor. In Sonnet 2/I, for example, the octet portrays the arrival of dawn and the manner in which its presence converts the horror of night into joy. There is no reference at all to the poet's lady. Suddenly, in line 9, the poet's purpose is made clear with the comparative 'tal,' and attention now shifts rapidly and forcefully to the importance and beauty of the beloved. The poet's objective has been not simply to eulogize his lady's splendour, but to do it in as striking a way as possible. The use of 'como' or 'cual' would have greatly lessened the dramatic quality by forewarning the reader that the initial description was but a prelude.

On other occasions Torre reveals his condition or feelings by contrast (in Book I, Sonnets 1, 18, 19, Ode 5; in Book II, Sonnet 9, Ode 2, or he invites comparisons by establishing a close relationship between himself and the objects that he addresses; for example, Ariadne in Endecha 6: 'Tú fuiste querida / y oluidada fuiste, / yo, querido y triste / quien me amó me oluida'; or Echo, in Eclogue 3: 'Tú conmigo también, Eco doliente, / ayunta tus querellas con las mías' (lines 91–92). The turtle-dove, nightingale, oak tree, and ivy were other favourite objects with which he associates his feelings in this manner.

Sometimes a hyperbole appears where the comparative 'tal' or 'assí' might be expected, as, for example, in stanza 37 of Eclogue I:

La bella ninfa Primauera y Flora
de flores cubren el marchito prado:
vna le viste y otra le colora,

vna de verde y otra de encarnado:
mas no tan presto sale mi pastora
dando su luz a todo lo criado,
quando del resplandor hermoso della
cubierta queda su presencia bella.

The description of the arrival of Primauera and Flora and of the joy and beauty associated with their presence recalls that of the advent of Aurora in Sonnet 2/I. Here, however, instead of equating Cintia's arrival with nature's forces, Títiro sees them as being surpassed by her. (This type of exaggeration coincides, of course, with the godlike qualities with which the lady is so often invested in Torre's verse.)

If Torre is a reluctant advocate of the normal simile, he more than compensates for it with his penchant for the simile 'más ... que,' a form that María Rosa Lida traces back to classical writers, especially Virgil.[26] Nevertheless, although Garcilaso used 'más ... que' with a fair degree of frequency (sixteen times), it was not practised so readily by the majority of sixteenth-century Spanish poets. Boscán avoids it entirely; Diego Hurtado de Mendoza employs it six times; Acuña, four times; Cetina but once; Vadillo, five times. In the second half of the sixteenth century, Laynez is sparing in his use of this simile and Silvestre employs it five times. Both Montemayor and Gil Polo are infrequent users of the device, as is Herrera. Only Francisco de Figueroa seems to be attracted with any degree of regularity to 'mas ... que,' which appears in his poetry twenty-seven times, the same number of times as in Torre's.

Francisco de la Torre adds nothing startling to the device, although he does incorporate it three times into a bipartite or parallelistic framework (Sonnet 8/II; Eclogue 1, stanza 18; and Eclogue 2, stanza 4). Unlike Figueroa he never employs for additional emphasis the adverb 'muy' nor the form 'mucho más ... que.' The imagery that is invariably used in this kind of simile (and that by custom, refers to the lady) appears to follow the traditional path. Comparisons are with light or objects of light, including the sun, the heavens, dawn, or with unfeeling or potentially violent aspects of nature, such as rocks, winds, ice, snow, mountains, and the sea.

Metaphor

Of all the poetic devices that form the hallmark of *culteranismo*, the metaphor was perhaps the most overused and abused. Handled by Góngora its impact was profound, if not always appreciated; in the hands of the incompetent, the metaphor gave ready ammunition to its detractors. There is no doubt that for

Quevedo and Vander Hammen, one of the attractions of Torre's verse was the very modest use the poet made of the metaphor. Apart from the metaphoric descriptions of feminine beauty in Eclogue 6, stanza 9 and Sonnet 11/1 (very brief), there is nothing to distinguish descriptions of his lady by Torre from those by his sixteenth-century contemporaries. He follows the Petrarchan tradition although, like Garcilaso, he does avoid the associations of lips with rubies or coral, teeth with pearls, and hands or arms with ivory that were so much in fashion in the second half of the sixteenth century.

The Petrarchan model was realistically described by neither Petrarch nor his imitators, but neither was the pastoral environment in which she moved. Within this bucolic paradise the presence of, or references to, mythological deities and figures (the 'diosas,' 'ninfas,' 'náyades') do not seem absurd. Nevertheless, while pagan myths are frequently alluded to in Garcilaso's verse, his descriptions of natural phenomena – sun, moon, wind, dawn – are very restricted. Torre, on the other hand, almost invariably converts these phenomena into their mythological equivalents, reflecting thereby a tendency of the second half of the sixteenth century. Such a procedure fits in with the evasion of reality implicit in the literary pastoral tradition.

If Garcilaso's descriptions of the sun are compared with those by Torre, the difference will be immediately evident. In Garcilaso's verse, 'Apolo' appears five times (all in Eclogue 3) and 'Febo' six times (all in Eclogue 2). However, despite the fact that these names were common classical allusions to the sun, only once (in Eclogue 2, line 911) is the mythological name applied to the sun. It is evident from the number of times that the noun 'sol' appears (of the thirty noted by Sarmiento, twenty-seven refer to the natural phenomenon)[27] that Garcilaso simply did not conceive of the sun in mythological terms.

In Francisco de la Torre's poetry, on the other hand, the sun's mythological equivalents, 'Apolo' or 'Febo,' dominate. But that is not all. Other allusions to the sun also occur which do not appear in Garcilaso: 'el reluciente dios dorado' (Eclogue 8, stanza 16), the 'pastor bello de Anfriso' (Ode 3/1, stanza 10), 'claro padre de Faetón' (Sonnet 32/11), 'la ... lámpara del Oriente luminoso' (Canción 1/1, stanza 6), 'la luz a quien sigue Diana' (Eclogue 2, stanza 2), the 'claro amante de Clicie' (Eclogue 4, stanza 10), 'el hijo soberano de Latona' (Eclogue 5, stanza 3), and 'el dios de Delo' (Eclogue 6, stanza 8).

Just as the sun is regularly convertd by Torre into a mythological metaphor, so too the moon is transformed into 'Diana' or 'Cintia.' Dawn is 'Aurora,' thunder is viewed as the activity of Jupiter, the rainbow is 'Iris,' and the winds are metamorphized into 'Aeolus,' 'Boreas,' 'Eurus,' 'Notus,' 'Auster,' or 'Favonius.' The difference between Torre and Garcilaso is again confirmed if it is recalled that many of the above terms (such as 'Cintia,' 'Aeolus,' 'Boreas' simply do not occur in the latter's verse; Garcilaso does, for example, refer to 'viento' thirty times but only once (in Eclogue 3, stanza 41) is a mythological equivalent ('Favonius') used.

Even geographical expanse or the passage of time may be couched in mythological terms in Torre's work. In Endecha 2 the lonely shepherd weeps day and night: 'Solo y pensativo / le halla el claro Febo. / Sale su Diana, / y hállale gimiendo.' In Canción 1/I the turtle-dove is advised: 'Llora, desventurada, llora quando / vieres resplandecer la soberana / lámpara del Oriente luminoso, / quando su blanca hermana / muestra su rostro blando.' In Sonnet 32/II the prosaic 'cualquier parte' or equivalent is converted to: 'En cuanto la sagrada lumbre / del claro padre de Faetón alcança,' a description echoed in Eclogue 1, stanza 3: 'A la más agradable y fértil vega / que el Ganges baña ni descubre Apolo.'

One final observation is that some of the above examples also point to an increased invasion of reality which prefigures a technique much practised by *culto* poets, namely allusions to allusions. A simple metaphor, such as 'Febo' or 'Diana,' in which there is a single, direct relationship between the real sun or moon and the myth, would pose no problems to the cultured reader of the Golden Age and quite soon would lose its poetic impact. References, however, to 'el dios de Delo' or 'el hijo soberano de Latona,' for instance, do not allude directly to the sun but to Apollo, and therefore only indirectly to the sun. The results of such indirect allusions – especially if an allusion is obscure or combined with others – are that the reader is placed at a greater mental distance from the object and that the intellectual demand made of him is increased. To be sure, the attempts at indirect references by Torre are modest (the most prolonged and complicated being the description of 'Aurora' in Ode 3/I), but the frequency with which those allusions occur and his evident interest in converting natural phenomena into the activities of classical deities show Torre to be no mere imitator of Garcilaso.[28] The mythological references or allusions also confirm the impression that his world is much more animated than Garcilaso's. Recall not only the constant presence of nymphs and deities, but also the arrival of Spring – invariably seen as 'Flora,' 'Primavera,' or 'Natura' – who moves about 'bordando' and 'texiendo,' or the change of weather, viewed as the anger of Arturus. As I have argued in the preceding chapter, the static vision of Arcadia is giving way to the animation of the baroque.

Recurrent Images

The images that I have in mind here (arboreal, animal, and bird) have been discussed to some degree in Chapters 1 and 2. Torre distinguishes himself from other sixteenth-century Spanish poets by the attention that he devotes to the suffering of these creatures, to such an extent that they become the protagonists of the poems.

Arboreal images, although introduced to Spain by Garcilaso, were used but once by him and their popularity for much of the sixteenth century was limited. They appear once in the works of Diego Hurtado de Mendoza, but not at all in those of Acuña, Cetina, Vadillo, Montemayor, Gil Polo, or Pedro Laynez. Torre, on the other hand, introduces arboreal images in ten of his poems, his major contribution being, as we have seen, in Canción 1/II and Canción 2/I. In each of these poems the natural objects are endowed with human qualities of love and suffering and, in a reversal of the traditional pattern, man's sorrow plays a secondary role. Certainly, to my knowledge no other Spanish poet of the sixteenth century portrays these objects of nature from such a personal point of view, or indeed, develops arboreal images into complete poems.

Of course, Torre does use this kind of image in the more traditional manner to symbolize reciprocal or unrequited love (Sonnet 5/II) or harmony (Eclogue 1, stanza 4; Eclogue 4, stanza 1). Ode 1/II contains a particularly splendid example of the artistic use of the image. The poem is a joyous vision of nature's annual rebirth, and is climaxed by a vision of the elm tree embraced by both the vine and the ivy:

Todo brota y estiende
ramas, hojas y flores, nardo y rosa,
la vid enlaza y prende
el olmo y la hermosa
yedra sube tras ella presurosa.

The image is particularly appropriate here. Literally, it fits in with the general description and 'binds together,' as it were, the series of visual images of the preceding strophes. Symbolically, the union of the vine and ivy with the elm reflects the highest form of harmony in the natural world, and it is immediately following this most explicit expression of mutual dependence that the poet suddenly and dramatically directs our attention to his isolation with the words: 'Yo, triste ...'

Torre, like those Spanish poets who do use arboreal images, appears unaware of the original Catullan distinction between the elm/vine and ivy/tree symbols.[29] However, unlike many of his compatriots (for example, Silvestre, Aldana, or Diego Hurtado de Mendoza), he is careful to avoid using these images to allude to physical embrace (see note 27, Chapter 1).

Unlike the arboreal image, that of the wounded stag had a twofold origin, Virgilian and biblical, which made it a vehicle of expression in both secular and religious verse. Sixteenth-century Spanish poets often fused the Virgilian and biblical images, although the Virgilian element, by virtue of its length, usually predominated. The wounded-stag image appears in Boscán, and is practised by Garcilaso, Cetina, Herrera, Fray Luis de León, and San Juan de la Cruz, among others.[30] However, with the exception of San Juan's 'Cántico espiritual,' nowhere is the image developed in such detail as in Torre's poetry. In Canción 2/II the image provides the subject-matter of the poem: the suffering of the hind is the only concern of the poet. Torre expands on the classical and biblical images: (1) concrete references to the hind's partner are added to the Virgilian simile; (2) the biblical brook conveys the idea not of refreshment but of death; (3) the hind, in her desire for death and union with her beloved, symbolizes the kind of fidelity associated with the turtle-dove (an association substantiated also, in stanza 4, by the simile 'como tórtolas solas y queridas'; and (4) the death of the hind and the beloved is seen as a kind of martyrdom and a triumphant release from mortal cares.

As a love symbol the image may even penetrate those poems with themes that are not amatory (Ode 4/I, stanza 1; Ode 3/II, stanza 4), although its normal use is to mirror the suffering arising out of love (as in Ode 6/I, Sonnet 31/II). However, as I have argued in Chapter 2, the erotic element is not pronounced. As in the arboreal simile, Torre does not evoke passionate images; he conveys, rather, an impression of regret at the unhappy separation of lover and beloved and does not dwell on the physical union.

The sorrow caused by the loss of a partner, illustrated by the arboreal and wounded-stag images, is reinforced by the third recurrent image in Torre's verse, that of the turtle-dove and/or nightingale. Again Torre devotes complete poems to the suffering of nature's creatures (Canción 1/I and Endecha 7, both dedicated to the turtle-dove), and the human element appears in a supporting role. As symbols of sorrow, without any erotic overtones, it is significant that they also appear in those poems in which the arboreal or animal objects are the protagonists (Canción 2/I, Canción 1/II, and Canción 2/II). Their presence substantiates the tragic aspect of those poems rather than the erotic.

The constant use of arboreal, animal, and bird imagery reflects something of Torre's sensitivity. '¿Hágote compañía con mi llanto?' he asks the turtle-dove, as if fearful of intruding upon the bird's suffering. Of course these images reveal human conditions, but Torre develops them and in so doing infuses new life into old *topoi*. This process corresponds too to the classical, anthropomorphic world that Torre creates. The stars also suffer; the night is an intimate friend; 'Flora' and 'Primavera' beautify the earth; Arturus and Jupiter can be destructive; and goddesses, nymphs, and deities abound. Is it surprising that trees, animals, and birds should have feelings of their own?

Vocabulary

(i) Cultismos

Seventeenth-century critics of *culteranismo* directed their anger not only at the syntactic complexities that characterized it but also at the abundance of neologisms and words borrowed from Latin, Italian, or any other source. Lorenço Vander Hammen, in particular, expresses his distaste for this practice in his 'Aprobación' to Francisco de la Torre's poetry. Attributing the demise of Hebrew to contamination by foreign words, he concludes that 'lo mismo pudiera dezir de la nuestra [lengua], porque casi hemos hecho de los vocablos ta[n]tas muda[n]ças como de la ropa, y podríamos hazer dos le[n]guas tan difere[n]tes, q[ue] el vno al otro no se entendiessen: porque nos damos tanta priessa a inuentar vocablos [o por dezirlo como ello es], a tomarlos prestados de otras lenguas, q[ue] por enriquecerla hemos de venir a desconocerla' (p. liii). The Castilian language, he continues, requires no cosmetic treatment; its virtues are to be found in 'el [lenguaje] que nos enseñaron nuestras madres y el que hablan en sus casas las castas matronas y mugeres bien criadas' (p. liii). Then, referring directly to Torre's poetry, he adds: 'En este [lenguaje], pues, está escrito este libro, aunque exornado co[n] todo lo que permite el arte' (p. liii).

Vander Hammen's assessment of Torre's language echoes the deep-rooted polemic that raged in Spain in the first half of the seventeenth century. Certainly, an enormous gap separates Torre's vocabulary from the lexical splendour of Góngora, or from Quevedo, the ardent critic of *culto* extravagance. Torre's vocabulary belongs essentially to the tradition of Garcilaso and the pastoral genre, although, as is to be expected in view of observations made regarding landscape scenes and, to a lesser extent, some of the metaphoric descriptions of the lady, it is by no means as restricted as that of the Toledan poet. The following partial list (omitting all mythogical names or allusions) contains, for example, words that do not appear in Garcilaso's verse:

abrasar, adorar, acopadas, alboradas, aljofarado, ambrosia, arenales, auecillas, bordar, brotar, caberna, concabidades, cóncabo, copiosas, coral, coro, criar (used to describe a natural scene), cueua, deidad, deshojar, ébano, empinada, enguirnaldar, esmeraldas, fértil, guirnalda, ídolo, impetuoso, inclemente, jacinto, orientales, ornar, ostro, perlas, plateado, pórfidos, púrpura, remoçar, resonar, rosada, rosicler, sonorosas, texer (used in landscape description), vmbría, vermejo, vestir (in landscape description), yerto.

The use of these words does not mean that Torre's poetry is more difficult to read than that of Garcilaso. They reflect, rather, something of the 'thematic' differences between Garcilaso and Torre, including, for example, the latter's deification of his lady and his varied landscape descriptions.

This lexical simplicity of Torre's verse does not mean, however, that it is of the kind that could be understood by the average person. The literary pastoral, by virtue of its tradition, belongs to 'poesía culta' with a restricted, educated audience. Consequently, the vocabulary of Torre's verse contains many *cultismos*, but they are not especially startling for they do not depart radically from the accepted bucolic stream. Even those words in Torre's work that are recorded by Alonso, Vilanova, and Kossoff as *cultismos* in the poetry of Góngora and Herrera would have been unlikely to offer serious problems for late sixteenth-century and early seventeenth-century readers.[31] The following list does not pretend to be exhaustive, but it does illustrate the kind of *cultismos* used by Torre:

acanto, admirar, adorar, alterar, amensar, amante, ambrosia, arder, argenta, áspero, áspid, aurora, ausente, ave, bello, blando, canción, cauerna, charo, cóncauo, coro, coronado, cristal, crudo, deidad, diuino, dulce, eclipsar, errante, espíritu, extremo, fábula, fértil, frágil, furor, gentil, gloria, honor, horizonte, horrendo, ídolo, impetuoso, injusto, inmenso, máchina, mirto, náufrago, nave, néctar, ninfa, nube, obscuro, ofrenda, ofuscar, pensamiento, plantas, plátano, púrpura, purpúreo, resplandeciente, rigor, sacrificio, sacro, sagrado, salve, sirena, sonorosa, suave, suspirar, tempestad, tempestuoso, templo, tesoro, tirano, transformar, vmbroso, veneno, violento.

Of the *cultismos* found in Torre's poetry, one – the superlative termination '-ísimo' – appears consistently. Margherita Morreale, in her work on Boscán's translation of Castiglione's *Cortegiano*, has observed that there is a notable increase in the use of the absolute superlative in the second half of the sixteenth century, a comment that is supported by Keniston in his work on the syntax of Castilian prose in the sixteenth century.[32] Menéndez Pidal emphasizes its *culto* origin: 'El superlativo "-issimo" se conservó en "-ísimo," forma enteramente culta y apenas usada en la Edad Media.'[33] While such observations help to reinforce the probability that Francisco de la Torre was a poet of the second half of the sixteenth century, it must not be assumed that all poets of this period made such liberal use of the superlative. There are forty-six examples in Torre's verse but only seven in the poetry of Herrera. Even smaller use is made by Medrano, whose work contains but one example. The *Diana* of Montemayor has sixty-one examples, fifty-three in the prose and eight in the verse. (Montemayor's *Cancionero* shows only one example!) The *Diana enamorada* of Gil Polo shows an increased use of the superlative, fifty-two occasions in the prose and twenty-eight in the poetry. Aldana employs it infrequently, as does Fray Luis de León. Of the poets whose works were consulted, only Laynez exceeds Torre, with a total of fifty-six examples in his verse.

In Torre's poetry, the majority of the superlatives in '-ísimo' appear in the eclogues, and there is a complete absence in the *endechas* and odes. Of the forty-six examples, thirty-six correspond with the sixth-syllable stress position, conveying thereby a pronounced rhythmic or musical quality to the poetry. Superlatives of adjectives referring to suffering or to the qualities of the beloved predominate: 'grauíssimo' nine times, 'bellíssimo' and 'duríssimo' each five times, and 'tristíssimo,' 'puríssimo,' and 'dulcíssimo' each four times. Sometimes the superlative increases the inherent quality of a noun or adverb (as in 'escuríssima noche,' Sonnet 2/1; 'grauíssimo mal,' Eclogue 3, line 25; and 'tristíssimas querellas,' Eclogue 7, stanza 1); sometimes it accentuates an oxymoron (for example, 'caríssimo enemigo,' Sonnet 3/1).

The recurrence of the absolute superlative brings to mind also the repeated presence of proparoxytonic words (that is, 'esdrújulos') in Torre's work. The result is similar to that of the absolute superlative, providing, in Dámaso Alonso's words, 'una musical alternancia de acentuación, y cuando recibe el acento rítmico, refuerza la expresión de todo el verso.'[34]

(ii) Polyptoton

In his commentary on Garcilaso's use of the verb 'acabar' (in the sonnet 'Cuando me paro a contemplar mi estado'), Herrera remarks that 'este verbo repetido cuatro veces con variación de tiempo sirve en lugar de la figura polítoton ..., y no como piensan algunos es aquí vicio, sino hermosísima virtud de la oración ...'[35] Although the play on words was a feature of Spanish *cancionero* poetry, Herrera's praise of its use was no doubt due to the involvement of the *ingenio* and to the exercise of the intellect. In a sense, word play is involved in epanalepsis or its variants (for example, 'Suspiro de contino y suspirando,' Sonnet 2/ II), but there are other examples in Torre's verse that would undoubtedly have met with Herrera's approval:

> Si el bien *passo* mi sentimiento blando,
> ni mal *passa* mi fuerte sufrimiento;
> si lo que recebí fue soberano,
> el mal que *passo passa* el ser humano.   (Eclogue 5, stanza 14)

> Después que la [vida] desamas
> *viua* y en *viuas* llamas   (Ecologue 6, stanza 15)

> Las sinrazones de las cosas *justas*
> en las *injustas* ánimas *injustas*   (Eclogue 6, stanza 36)

> *Falta* la voz el ánimo cansado
> y *faltara* la *vida* juntamente,
> si fuera *falta* para ser sentida.
> Bien se pareze como *viuo* ausente
> de quien *viuir* presente y apartado
> es muerte fiera y es alegre *vida*.   (Eclogue 8, stanza 7)

> Agora que me tienes apartado
> de la beldad que admira cielo y suelo
> me das a conocer el *bien perdido*.
> *Bien* sé que con *perder* vn *bien* del cielo
> en quien se muestra su valor cifrado,
> quedé, más que *perdido* entristecido.   (Eclogue 8, stanza 8)

(iii) Adjectives with 'Mal'

Dámaso Alonso has noted the great use made by Francisco de Medrano of adjectives formed with the adverb 'mal.' 'Quizá,' says Alonso, 'no haya una afectación de léxico que sea más repetida ni más característica de Medrano que el empleo de adjetivos compuestos con el adverbio "mal".'[36] On occasion the model is clearly Horace, although, as Alonso adds, 'ha podido pesar en Medrano el ejemplo literario de Italia.'[37] Alonso also draws attention to the presence of these adjectives in the verse of some of Medrano's contemporaries, such as Herrera, Soria Galvano (a friend), and Fray

Luis de León. Although Torre did not use adjectives preceded by 'mal' as consistently as Medrano, his name also could have been added to Alonso's list. The following appear in his work:

Bienes dudosos, mal seguidas glorias	(Sonnet 9 I)
Aguda roca y mal seguro seno	(Sonnet 10/I)
... vna mal segura lumbre clara	(Sonnet 19/II)
Ellos mal concertados y auenidos	(Sonnet 29/II)
Tan mal pagado amor, tan gran tormento	(Sonnet 32/II)
... tus atreuimientos mal regidos	(Ode 4/II, stanza 4)
Las imitadas mal seguras alas	(Ode 4/II, stanza 5)
Los mal regidos súbditos del fiero / Eolo	(Ode 4/II, stanza 9)
Su mal acontecido pensamiento	(Eclogue 5, stanza 6)

The fact that the superlative '-íssimo' or adjectives with 'mal' stand out as *cultismos* in Torre's verse indicates his lexical modesty. Although they reflect interesting aspects of his style, they could scarcely be considered startling innovations; they constitute, really, an intensified use of already existing forms. And even the polyptota are a prolongation of a firmly established tradition in Spanish poetry.

Two final *cultismos* should also be mentioned, although their role in Torre's poetry is limited: the single verb with plural subject and *tmesis* (a device whereby a word, split at the end of one line of poetry, is continued at the beginning of the following line). The following examples of a single verb with plural nouns may be observed in Torre's verse:

Resplandeció el Oriente y el Ocaso	(Sonnet 4/I)
Iris resplandeció y el cielo sacro	(Sonnet 25/II)
Yace muriendo viuo el temerario Enzélado y Tipheo	(Ode 4/II, stanza 6)
Y al punto que la encierra en su concha espaciosa Glauco, y Tetis hermosa	(Canción 3/II, stanza 1)
Cuya serenidad y cuya humana presencia mansa y mansedumbre tierna ofrece paz, descanso y gloria ofrece	(Eclogue 1, stanza 17)
Faltó la voz y vida juntamente	(Eclogue 2, stanza 21)[38]

Of *tmesis* there are but two instances in Torre's work:

Voy tan confuso y mustio, que ordinaria-
mente me llaman ...   (Sonnet 14/II)

Y tendiendo ligera-
mente el rayo diuino   (Eclogue 2, stanza 17)

In the appendix to Quevedo's edition of Torre's poetry, Juan de Almeida defends the use of *tmesis*. He recalls its presence not only in Fray Luis de León, but also in Ariosto and Horace; it is, he concludes, a poetic licence 'autorizada y enriquecida con los escritos de hombres tan doctos' (p. 203).[39]

Aesthetic Contrast

It is a common observation that throughout our lives we are in constant contact with, or are made aware of, opposing physical forces, such as light and darkness, movement and repose, and violence and peace. And this awareness is provided not only by our senses; our mental faculties too inform us of the existence of such moral or intellectual opposites as good and evil, past and future, and love and hate. Without these opposing forces life as we understand it would be highly monotonous and, to most, meaningless.

Art (in its most general sense) too requires the constant interplay of opposites, awakening not only the delight of the senses but also the appreciation of the intellect. Garcilaso suggests an awareness of nature's aesthetic appeal when he refers to the banks of the Tagus as 'alegrando la hierba (vista?) y el oído.'[40] Nevertheless, his descriptions of the natural world are primarily literary and contain very restricted or subdued contrasts, as befitted the classical *locus amoenus*. Aesthetic contrast in the poetry of Francisco de la Torre, however, reflects a marked difference from that of his illustrious predecessor. In Eclogue 2, for example, following Tirsi's lament and suicide – both of which take place during the night – stanzas 15 and 16 offer differing descriptions of an identical location. This contrast is the result of a very rapid, violent transformation of night into day, darkness into light and colour (emphasized by enumeration), noise into silence, and violent action into ordered movement. Such an abrupt change is foreign to the type of landscape established by Garcilaso and, rather than looking backward to his static Arcadia, it points forward to the baroque love of contrasts.

An equally startling transformation, without the auditory contrast, may be observed in stanzas 16 and 17 of Eclogue 5. After numerous stanzas that are completely devoid of colour and devoted entirely to the complaint of the forlorn Palemón, the dazzling colours spread over the world by Aurora constitute a 'claroscuro' that compares favourably with that of any poet of the

Golden Age. Torre's awareness of the artistic effect of contrast is alluded to by the fact that the opening stanzas of the poem portray an aqueous locale surrounded by sun-scorched fields. Then in order to emphasize the aesthetic opposition between night and dawn, Torre transforms the scene entirely with the lines 'Blancas, purpúreas flores produziendo, / prados, valles, montes aljofarando.'

The contrasts in the above passage arise from the desire to depict the metamorphosis of night into day. Other instances may be adduced that are not dependent on sudden temporal transformations. The opening stanzas of Eclogue 6 provide us with a remarkable visual contrast of depth and height, together with implied contrasts of noise and silence and of movement and repose. From the rapid movement of the water at the foot of the 'rocas' we are suddenly transported up towards the heavens, to the silent world of snow-covered mountains. Not only is the inhospitality of this remote setting evoked alien to the pastoral world, but the change of visual perspective also marks a radical departure from the traditional scenes.

Stanza 20 of Eclogue 4 provides a contrast in sound and movement. A mountain stream, having nourished the 'alameda fresca,' rapidly increases its speed and noisily hurtles down the mountain-side, 'haziendo vn ronco son de peña en peña,' until 'en el sagrado río se despeña.' From this rapid movement we are conveyed abruptly back to the 'fuente' by which Tirsi and a nymph seat themselves. Quickly the roaring noise gives way to the subdued complaints of the lovers, and the swift movement of the waters to the immobility of the pastoral figures.

The baroque love of contrast is also to be seen in the sweeping visions and changes of perspective. Stanza 3 of Eclogue 2, for example, contains a highly compressed but sweeping view of 'sunfall' and 'nightrise' as counter balancing and simultaneous actions: 'Al tiempo que la noche tenebrosa / iba subiendo por el rojo Oriente, / y el claro Dios al mar se despenaua, / matizando las nubes de Occidente.'

The background descriptions of Eclogues 4 and 8 illustrate the contrast between the general and the particular. The initial stanza of Eclogue 4 portrays a large-scale picture of the banks of the river Tesín enveloped in colour. Stanza 2, however, immediately focuses on a specific spot, the 'concabidades de vna piedra,' where the shepherd, Tirsi, is to appear. In Eclogue 8, the first strophe provides a general picture of an autumn dawn, filled with light, colour, and the joyous music of birds. Stanza 2 transfers us to Montano's cave, an isolated spot, cool, shady, and silent.

In Eclogue 1 the procedure is reversed and the forlorn Palemón is the object of attention in the first stanzas. Focus then moves to the banks of the

Tagus, crowned with flowers, and the forest swaying gently in the breeze. (One might also consider stanza 7 an example of the particular within the general, as the poet momentarily concentrates on a nightingale perched in one of the trees.)

Eclogue 5 combines the procedure of Eclogue 1 (moving from the particular to the general) with the rapid change of perspective (from sea-level to mountain peaks) of Eclogue 6. From the secluded 'lugar' of line 1 the picture changes swiftly to a panoramic vision and carries the reader abruptly from the confluence of the Tagus with the sea to 'los más leuantadas Orizontes.'

The abrupt contrasts, the sudden and rapid changes of perspective, the sweeping visions occur only in the eclogues, and exclusively in the landscape descriptions. There is no doubt that in his observance of the natural world, his aesthetic interest, and his artistic use of contrast to portray his vision, Torre represents an important stage in the poetic trajectory from Garcilaso to Góngora.

Colour

In view of my remarks about Torre's treatment of nature and use of contrast, that his verse shows a greater wealth of colour than that of Garcilaso should not be surprising. Nevertheless, with the exception of the colour red, there is a relatively similar frequency of colour adjectives in the works of both poets. Margot Arce points out that Garcilaso used 'verde' forty times, 'blanco' thirty-nine, 'oro-rubio' twenty-six, 'rojo-colorado' and 'rosa' each six times 'amarillo' and 'negro' each four times, and 'marfil,' 'plata,' and 'azul' once each.[41] In Torre's poetry 'verde' appears thirty-seven times, 'blanco-neuado-plateado' thirty-eight, 'oro-dorado' twenty-four, 'colorado-encarnado-purpúreo' forty-one, 'rojo' twenty-three times, 'purpúreo' nine, 'negro' six, 'rojado' four, 'azul' and 'pardo' twice each, and 'amarillo' once. In view of the greater frequency of red, the colour contrast red-white, used four times by Garcilaso, is increased to fourteen in Torre. Another colour combination for which Torre shows some preference is that of red-green, which appears five times.

Nevertheless, the colour adjectives themselves are not the only elements that convey chromatic wealth; if such were the case there would not be much difference between Garcilaso and Torre.[42] It is the details of the landscape – the trees, the fields, the riverbanks – that impart the chromatic characteristics in the poetry of each. In Garcilaso's case the colour that dominates is a pale, subdued green with only a hint of red here and there; in Torre's poetry, the green is substantially stronger, thanks to the activities of 'Flora,' 'Primavera,' and 'Natura'; and the touches of red more pronounced (for example, Eclogue 2, stanza 1; Eclogue 4, stanza 1; Eclogue 1, stanzas 4 and 8). In addition, we should keep in mind the evocative power of other words that increase the impression of nature's wealth. In Eclogue 2, in addition to Flora and Natura, there are 'arenales puros de oro,' 'acopadas plantas,' and 'hermosura de Arabia,' as well as the gerunds 'bordando,' 'descubriendo,' and 'texiendo.' The first stanza of Eclogue 4 contains 'Primavera,' 'belleza,' 'flores,' 'colores,' 'plantas,' 'hojas,' 'arboleda,' and the gerunds 'coronando,' 'bordando,' 'vistiendo,' and 'entretexiendo.' Eclogue 8 opens with references to 'rosicler,' 'perlas Orientales ... esmaltadas,' 'colores variadas,' 'pintadas aves,' and 'plantas amenissimas.'

In spite of Zamora Vincente's opinion that 'No hay apenas composición de la Torre donde no aparezcan elementos de color' (pp. xxxv–xxxvi), it would be an exaggeration to assume that almost all Torre's verse is sprinkled with colour. Many of the sonnets, odes, *canciones*, and *endechas* contain little or no chromatic variety, and it is pertinent to recall that the 'action' of five of the eclogues takes place at night, which restricts the 'preocupación pictórica' that Zamora considers 'permanente, exaltada' (p. xxxv). Likewise, there are scenes that are largely aqueous or stormy in nature, and the monologues of the shepherds are remarkably devoid of colour. What, then, is the criterion for considering that Torre's verse contains more sensorial wealth than that of Garcilaso? The answer lies in features of Torre's style, principally in his considerable use of contrast, enumeration (often together with repetition), and the accumulative effect of subordinate clauses. Furthermore, contrast need not be limited to brief opposition of individual colours in the fashion of Garcilaso, but may also illustrate the baroque principle of dissimilar scenes. In Torre's verse these scenes are based on the opposition of light and darkness (Eclogues 2 and 5) or simply on passages containing colour followed by numerous stanzas that offer little or no chromatic variety (Eclogues 1, 2, 4, and 8). Torre is still distant from the Góngora of the *Polifemo* and *Soledades* (or from Pedro Espinosa, for that matter) in that he does not constantly employ colour-evoking words, but his landscape descriptions do reveal a much greater aesthetic awareness of Nature's variety – its composition and form – than those of Garcilaso.

Versification

Torre's mannerisms and his attempts to capture stylistic features of classical writers are complemented by a similar orientation in versification, as witnessed by his use of the *lira* (Odes 1/I, 4/I and 1/II), the *cuarteto-lira* (Odes 3/I and 3/II), and especially the *estrofa de la Torre* (Odes 2/I and 2, 4, and 5/II). The *lira*, a five-lined stanza consisting of a combination of hendecasyllables and heptasyllables with a rhyme scheme of aBabB (the capital letters indicate the hendecasyllables), was introduced into Spain by Garcilaso. Garcilaso's inspiration was the sixteenth-century Italian poet, Bernardo Tasso, who sought, in Dámaso Alonso's words, 'una oda apta para las rápidas transiciones horacianas.'[43] The increased use of the *lira* in the second half of the sixteenth century, especially among writers associated with Salamanca, attests to the popularity of Horace in the university town during this period. Although they were by no means the only source of inspiration, Horace's themes – the brevity of life, the peace of the countryside, the rapid changeability of fortune – appeared to have had a certain affinity with the sensibility of the poets of Salamanca.

The *cuarteto-lira*, which made its appearance in the second half of the sixteenth century, is a four-line strophe with a combination of alternating hendecasyllables and heptasyllables rhyming AbAb or aBaB (the former being the only paradigm used by Torre). In Baehr's opinion 'se aproximó más a los tipos principales de la estrofa de la oda horaciana que la lira de Garcilaso ...'[44] Its use by poets connected with Salamanca – Fray Luis de León and Francisco de Medrano, in particular – reaffirms Horace as a source of inspiration in that town.

The *estrofa de la Torre* consists of three unrhymed hendecasyllables followed by a heptasyllable. It was created by Torre because, in Menéndez y Pelayo's opinion, 'no se satisfizo el bachiller de la Torre con sus cuartetos ...quiso llegarse a la métrica clásica y destruir la rima.'[45] More recently, Baehr has argued that the *estrofa de la Torre* imitates more closely the Horatian ode than the *lira* or *cuarteto-lira* precisely because of its lack of rhyme scheme. 'El autor pensó,' continues Baehr, 'más bien, en la creación de un tipo de estrofa propio para imitar las formas horacianas, que sin resultar extraño en la poesía de lengua vulgar, proporcionase, no obstante, cierta impresión como de oda horaciana.'[46]

Another interesting verse form employed by Torre, although not necessarily of classical origin, is that of the *heptasílabo suelto* (Odes 5 and 6/I), which appears to have been first attempted in Spain by the dramatist Jerónimo Bermúdez in his two best-known works *Nise lastimosa* and *Nise laureada* (both published in 1577). 'Hacia la misma fecha,' suggests Tomás Navarro, 'debió ser compuesta la oda en cuartetos de heptasílabos sueltos que Francisco de la Torre dejó entre sus imitaciones clásicas.'[47] Torre's blank heptasyllables differ from those of Bermúdez in that they consist (with the exception of the last eight lines of Ode 5/I) of four-line strophes. The possible origins of Torre's *heptasílabos sueltos* are difficult to determine. However, the fact that Bermúdez had been a student of theology at Salamanca, and a similarity of ideas between some of his verse and that of Torre, suggest that Bermúdez himself was Torre's inspiration or vice versa.[48] Or, very simply, the rejection of rhyme may have been inspired by Torre's experiments in unrhymed hendecasyllables (Eclogue 3; again an attempt, perhaps, to approximate classical metres) or combinations of unrhymed hendecasyllables and heptasyllables, as witnessed in the stanza form that bears his name.

The verse forms of Italian provenance that appear in his poetry, the sonnet, the *estancia*, and the *octava rima*, show that Torre deviated little from the established norms. As Sena has pointed out, Torre's sonnets never contain paradigms of two rhymes only in the sestets. All the paradigms are based on three rhymes, the most common being CDE : CDE (36 examples), followed by CDE : DCE (17), CDE : CED (5), CDE : EDC (3), CDE : ECD (2), CDE : DEC (1).[49]

The *estancia*, consisting of a variable combination of hendecasyllables and heptasyllables (the order of which and the number of lines that made up a stanza were always determined by the paradigm of the first strophe), is a vastly more flexible form than the sonnet, and Torre follows the established pattern of using it in his *canciones* and his eclogues (2, 4, 6, 7, and 8). Torre appears to offer no particular innovations, although one curious detail is that he is not averse to occasionally altering the stanza length within an eclogue with no clearly defined purpose.[50]

The *octava rima*, a stanza of eight hendecasyllabic lines rhyming ABABABCC, was used by Torre in Eclogues 1 and 5. The simplest structure of the *octava* tends to divide the eight lines into two symmetrical groups of four, with a possible further division after each pair of lines. Examples of the form in Torre's poetry include Eclogue 1 (stanzas 22, 25, 34, and 41) and Eclogue 5 (stanzas 6, 8, and 11). However as the sixteenth century progressed other characteristics were also incorporated. It became increasingly popular to end the *octava* with a *bimembre*, which in turn reflected the bipartite structure of the stanza:

The effect of such a structure, in Dámaso Alonso's view, is that of 'serenidad contrabalanceada, de equilibrio.'[51] Examples of this may be found in stanza 23 of Eclogue 1 and stanza 31 of Eclogue 5.

The bimembre, however, need not be restricted to the final line of the octave. Elsewhere, Alonso has noted that 'Frecuentemente surgen en la estrofa más relaciones binarias que las que contiene ese esquema [as outlined above].'[52] Such development, he argues, is characteristic of the baroque. He offers the following outline as an example:

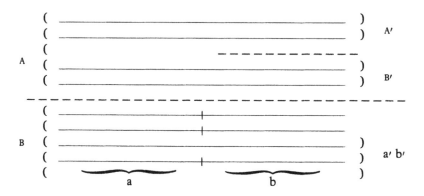

Although there are, to my knowledge, no identical structures in Torre's *octavas*, the following three outlines reflect a similar complexity:

Eclogue 1, stanza 5:

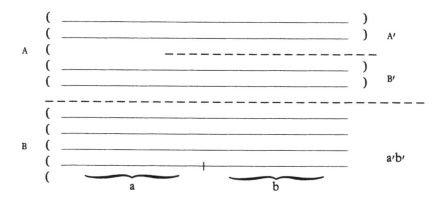

Eclogue 1, stanza 8:

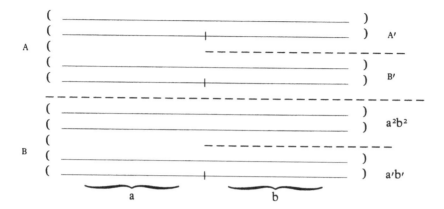

Eclogue 5, stanza 20:

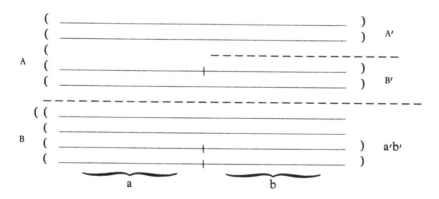

A cursory comparison between the *octavas* of Torre's two eclogues and Góngora's *Polifemo* will reveal how much more intensified and consistent is the latter's use of structural complexity. Nevertheless, although few, the above examples from Torre do illustrate the development of the *octava's* structure in the sixteenth century, especially in comparison with, for example, Boscán's 'octava rima,' Garcilaso's third eclogue, or Acuña's 'Fábula de Narciso.'

Of the other verse forms that he employed, the *redondilla menor* and the *romancillo*, Torre seems to have preferred the *redondilla menor*, since he used it in Endechas 1 and 3 to 10 and the *romancillo* in Endecha 2 only. The *redondilla menor*, a traditional Spanish metre consisting of strophes of four hexasyllabic lines rhyming abba (with a possible variation abab), enjoyed limited popularity in the sixteenth century. The one educated poet mentioned by both Navarro and Baehr as having used the form before Torre was Diego Hurtado de Mendoza, though it was abundantly used later by the Count of Villamediana and Pedro Quirós. It appears that Torre also anticipated seventeenth-century poets in introducing the *romancillo* into *poesía culta*. Evidence suggests that the acceptance of this traditional form (consisting of hexasyllabic lines with assonance in even lines) by educated poets took place only in the final third of the sixteenth century, but since it was used by Lope, Góngora, and Quevedo, its popularity obviously increased quickly.

Conclusion

In his *Agudeza y arte de ingenio* Gracián has occasion to insert one quotation from Francisco de la Torre's verse.[1] Given Gracián's *conceptista* orientation, it is not surprising that Torre's poetry should have had little appeal for him, and the example that he chooses (Canción 1/1) suffers by comparison with the selections from Góngora's work that immediately follow. Of course, in a sense it is unfair to compare Torre's verse with that of Góngora, and Gracián, rather than being critical of Torre, was more concerned with emphasizing the Cordoban's mastery of a particular poetic device. Torre clearly belongs to another, earlier age and his poetic vision is still largely governed by the cultural tastes of that age. The overwhelming majority of critics have seen him, as I have indicated in my introduction, as an imitator of Garcilaso and second only to Garcilaso as a pastoral poet, no mean judgment by any standard. But to call Torre an imitator and to dismiss him as only that, as if justice had been done thereby, is surely a hasty, albeit unintended, slight on his contribution.

Certainly, there will be no argument that Torre belongs, first and foremost, to the pastoral mould which, by its very nature, imposes certain restrictions. Its introduction into Spain, thanks to the genius of Garcilaso, was so remarkably successful that few if any later poets were able to remain indifferent to its pervasive influence, and Garcilaso became the esteemed Spanish model, equated with such luminaries as Virgil, Horace, and Petrarch. It is scarcely unexpected, therefore, that Torre should be indebted to his illustrious predecessor, but such a debt should not necessarily imply imitation, much less direct borrowing. Certainly the final line of stanza 3, Eclogue 6, 'que estoy muriendo y aun la vida temo,' is taken directly from line 60 of Garcilaso's first eclogue, and the line '¡O tiempo por mi mal rogado!' from Sonnet 18/1 may be an echo of Garcilaso's famous '¡O dulces prendas por mi mal halladas!' Apart from these two exceptions, however, there appears to be no evidence of immediate debt to Garcilaso.[2] Indeed, where direct imitation is concerned, Torre looked more to Italian sources than to Spanish – principally to Benedetto Varchi, Giovanni Battista Amaltheo, Giovanni Guidiccioni, Torquato Tasso, and Andrea Navagero – as Fucilla and others have shown.[3] And where general inspiration is concerned, there is no doubt that Horace was of some considerable importance, especially in the odes, and quite possibly in the creation of the 'estrofa de la Torre.'

Torre's imitation of Garcilaso is, then, for too limited for his verse to be reduced to a kind of second edition of the poetry of his illustrious predecessor, albeit a second edition with some 'puntos de vista personales,' as FitzMaurice-Kelly put it.[4] These 'puntos de vista personales' are more numerous than has been generally recognized. There is, for instance, a marked contradiction between Torre's Platonic utterances and his courtly propensities, which is of a more than passing interest. The Platonic tone of Sonnets 24 and 28/I and Sonnet 23/II is balanced by the courtly-Petrarchan orientation of Sonnets 10, 12, and 21/I, in a manner strongly reminiscent of Francisco de Aldana in some of his poems, although Torre's imagery is not as erotic as that of Aldana, or his Platonic expression as profound. But the Platonic courtly dichotomy is not limited to these particular sonnets. Torre's view of love ranges from unrequited suffering to an awareness, in a vague Platonic fashion, of the universal potential of love. Trees, animals, birds, and even the moon and stars share in this Platonic undercurrent of cosmic love, although it must be recognized that Torre does not consciously develop the philosophical content or the religious implications of this concept in the manner of Fray Luis de León and later writers. This view of potential universal love is predicated not on any statements that Torre makes to that effect, but on the fact that trees, animals, and various other objects suffer because love no longer exists, owing to the caprices of fate or to death or rejection. Torre's view, in this sense, is more romantic than that of sixteenth-century love poets whose vision is restricted more to personal suffering – à la Herrera – or, in the case of Pedro Laynez or Vadillo, to a rather academic definition of love.[5]

In the transposition of human emotions to natural and sometimes impersonal objects, there is a certain anthropomorphic quality, which is paralleled also in the activities of the gods and goddesses (for example, nereids, dryads, nymphs, Flora) who people Torre's poetic world. And the metamorphosis of so many common natural phenomena (such as the sun, winds, thunder, sea) into their classical equivalents, the humanizing of night and its shadowy companion, silence, confirm this anthropomorphic orientation in a manner that few, if any, Spanish poets of the sixteenth century can equal.

In this animated ambience, with its constant presence of classical deities, a creature of flesh and blood would seem singularly inappropriate, and Torre's lady is, as I have shown, no ordinary mortal. Her goddesslike qualities clearly place her in a polytheistic rather than monotheistic framework, and thereby outside the bounds of strict Platonism or Neo-Platonism (with the exception, of course, of Sonnets 24 and 28/1 and Sonnet 23/11). Though Torre may view love as a potential universal force, his attitude to his lady, his 'diosa,' shows more of the courtly-Petrarchan desire or frustration than the Plantonic joy of pure contemplation, and his poetry, as a whole, echoes a worldly, more than a spiritual, preoccupation. There is no contradiction between this earthly nature of Torre's desires and the revered qualities of his lady. She is adored, principally, for her physical beauty, and her divinity is intended to convey her immeasurable splendour and significance. In this sense Torre is more akin to Herrera than to Garcilaso, although the tension between the body and the soul is much more acute in Herrera's verse than it ever is in Torre's.

The shepherds of Torre's poetry are not moved to passionate extremes, although they are not slow to cry out against the vagaries of fate. Disillusioned, the lover may contemplate suicide, a topic that, in view of the religious temper of the day, was fraught with danger. Nevertheless, self-destruction is consummated on three occasions, twice in Eclogue 2 and once in Eclogue 6. The theological implications of such an act do not appear to have preoccupied Torre any more than other writers, such as Encina, Figueroa, or Laynez who touch upon the subject, and no attempt is made to dissuade the distraught lovers on religious or moral grounds. Possibly the fact that Torre did not enter into matters of faith, together with the prestige of the pastoral/mythological tradition (in which suicide was not unknown), made the suicides of Eclogues 2 and 6 acceptable to the Church. Certainly, neither Valdivielso nor Lorenço Vander Hamen in their respective 'aprobaciones' saw anything that contradicted or endangered the faith.

Irrespective of the tenor of a lover's complaint, the setting in which he was normally placed usually followed, in the pastoral, the traditional pattern of the classical *locus ameonus*. Although Torre does appear to have had a special interest in this natural background, perhaps more so than other sixteenth-century Spanish pastoral poets, it would be misleading to see nature as an independent 'theme' in his verse. In a recent work, M.J. Woods has argued correctly that, in the sixteenth century, 'to write poetry which sought first and foremost to describe nature ... meant in effect creating a new genre of poetry ...'[6] and the sixteenth century was not ready to undertake that step. As long as the natural descriptions were conditioned by a literary landscape, their function would be largely rhetorical and their visual evocation of secondary importance. The attention in this period is still focused on human relationships, and the descriptive background serves as a temporal or spatial framework for the thoughts of the lover or shepherd, especially in such longer poems as the eclogues and *canciones*. Even the occasional poet who does seem to have a topographic locale in mind, for example, Montemayor or Figueroa, never departs from the primary objective of expressing the lover's feelings. Similarly, Francisco de la Torre never downgrades in his poems the human interest in favour of nature but, by the same token – as I have attempted to show in chapter 3 – he is not satisfied to merely copy the established pattern of his time. I have outlined the differences, ranging from the 'romantic' view of nature's suffering creatures to the marked predilection for the *locus aquaticus*, from the isolated locale to the panoramic sweep encompassing mountains and sea, from the rebirth of spring to the scorched lands of summer. Here, indeed, Torre strikes out on his own, and no other Spanish poet of the sixteenth century, in so far as I am aware, expands the descriptive background so radically beyond the pleasance. The very length of some of the landscape descriptions betrays a greater interest, if not in nature itself, in elaborating upon long-standing motifs. We are still a long way from the sense of wonder and surprise that later poets saw in the various objects of nature – from the humblest flower to mighty forests – but Torre's world does point forward to the seventeenth century and not to the relatively static confines of earlier writers, such as Garcilaso.

Of course, when Quevedo published Torre's poetry, it was not with the intention of counteracting the *culterano* perception of nature; the purpose, substantiated by the censors Valdivielso and Vander Hammen, was to take aim at the linguistic ammunition of the *culteranistas*. Torre's greatest virtue was that he wrote plainly, so it seemed, and undoubtedly the approval of Quevedo and others rested on Torre's unambitious hyperbata and modest metaphors. In a sixteenth-century poet little else could be expected, given the importance attached to the pursuit of good models and the lack in Spain of poetic theories that would encourage a more radical approach. Herrera's well-known commentaries on Garcilaso's verse were not published until 1580, and they appear to have had no immediate repercussions, probably because of the well-established practice of searching for good models. (Six years before Herrera's *Anotaciones*, El Brocense could still proclaim: 'No tengo por buen poeta al que no imita los excelentes antiguos.')

The search for good models did not end, of course, with the advent of Góngora and his followers, but classical and Italian writers, rather than being models to be closely imitated, now became sources of inspiration, points of departure, and increasingly poets to be emulated. Herrera had decreed, as if he had in mind Juan de Valdés's well-known precept ('escribo como hablo'), that to write as one spoke was a poetic sin. The great models of antiquity and of Italy were not infallible in their treatment of various themes nor did they know all there was to know about style. Herrera does not dismiss the great models, but he does suggest that writers of his day should break the bondage of literary imitation and use their own inspiration. This challenge, of course, was not ignored by Góngora and his followers, although it is ironic that, in developing to the fullest the stylistic potential of sixteenth-century Spanish verse, they developed a more latinate syntax that was, in their minds, more elegant, more poetic. There is no evidence that Torre knew Herrera's thoughts on style and imitation, but his style reveals a writer of uncommon ability and innovation. His verse may not evoke the 'admiración' so desired by *culterano* writers, but certain of his stylistic devices – *bimembres* and epanalepsis, the accumulation of subordinate clauses, and the relative 'cuyo' come immediately to mind – show that he was already treading the path that later *culto* poets were to follow. Certainly neither Herrera nor his contemporaries seemed to have made such a conscious effort as did Torre to latinize their poetic syntax (witness the latinizing tendency of the verse form that bears the latter's name). Had Torre been more daring in his use of hyperbaton and metaphor, these other *culterano* traits would probably have already been recognized and his contribution more appreciated.[7]

Torre deserves more than amorphous generalizations about his sensitivity to nature or reiterated affirmations about his stylistic simplicity. In the development of Golden Age verse he should be recognized as an important transitional figure between Garcilaso and Góngora, an original artist who flowered quietly in a period of remarkable literary luxuriance.

Notes

INTRODUCTION

1 See Francisco de la Torre *Poesías*, edited by Alonso Zamora Vicente. (Madrid: Espasa-Calpe 1956). This is the edition (a reissue of Zamora's 1944 edition) that I have used, and all references to the introduction, the poems, and the appendix of this edition will be made in the text. For the sake of brevity, poems in the first two books are identified by the Roman numerals I or II, immediately following the Arabic number, e.g., Sonnet 10/I.

2 Enriqueta Terzano 'Un poeta no identificado: Francisco de la Torre' *Nosotros* 13: 93–8, and Peter M. Komanecky 'Quevedo's Notes on Herrera: the Involvement of Francisco de la Torre in the Controversy over Góngora' *BHS* 52: 123–33

3 The reasons for Quevedo's hostility and the way in which he proceeded to attack Herrera are very well detailed in Komanecky's article.

4 Manuel Faria y Sousa, ed. *Lusiadas de Luis de Camoens* vol. I (Lisbon: Imprenta Nacional–Casa de Moeda 1972) 75

5 Lope de Vega 'El Laurel de Apolo' *BAE* 38: 200

6 Ibid., 200

7 See Torre *Poesías* p. xi, fn. 1 (continued on p. xii).

8 Aureliano Fernández-Guerra y Orbe 'Francisco de la Torre' in *Discursos leídos ante la Real Academia Española* (Madrid: Rivadeneyra 1857) 6–51

9 Ibid., 8

10 Ibid., 11

11 Ibid., 13–14

12 Adolphe Coster 'Sur Francisco de la Torre,' *RHi* 65: 74–132

13 J.P.W. Crawford 'Francisco de la Torre and Juan de Almeida' *MLN* 42: 365–71. Crawford, like Coster, had also published in 1925 an article on

Torre entitled 'Francisco de la Torre y sus poesías' *Homenaje a Menéndez Pidal* vol. 2 (Madrid: Hernando 1925) 431–46.

14 Crawford 'Francisco de la Torre and Juan de Almeida' *MLN* 42: 369
15 Ibid., 370
16 Narciso Alonso Cortés 'Algunos datos sobre Hernando de Acuña y Francisco de la Torre' *HR* 9: 41–7
17 Jorge de Sena *Francisco de la Torre e D. João de Almeida* (Paris: Centro Cultural Português 1974)
18 Ibid., 191
19 There should be no confusion between the Bachiller Francisco de la Torre and Francisco de la Torre y Sevil, Caballero del Hábito de Calatrava, who was born around 1615 in Tortosa and was well-known in the literary circles of Saragossa until his death in 1682. A poet and dramatist, Torre y Sevil is probably best known now as an epigrammatist and Spanish translator of the Anglo-Welsh poet John Owen. Confusion does exist however. An example can be found in the General Index of the *Biblioteca de Autores Españoles*, vol. 71, 331, where a *romancillo*, 'El pastor más triste,' by the Bachiller is grouped with poems by Francisco de la Torre y Sevil. Even a recent and highly respected manual of Spanish literature makes the error of incorporating in its bibliography of the sixteenth-century poet an article referring to the seventeenth-century Torre. See J.L. Alborg *Historia de la literatura española* 2d ed., vol. 1 (Madrid: Gredos 1970) 833.
20 Faria y Sousa, ed. *Lusiadas de Luis de Camoens* 136
21 Leandro Fernández de Moratín *Obras póstumas* vol. 2 (Madrid: Rivadeneyra 1867), 'Carta a don Juan Bautista Conti' 118
22 Manuel José Quintana *Poesías selectas castellanas* vol. 1 (Madrid: Fuentenebros y Compañía 1807) xxxix–xlii
23 Ibid., xli
24 Ibid., xli
25 Ibid., xlii
26 George Ticknor *History of Spanish Literature* vol. 2 (New York: Harper & Brothers 1849) 264, 266
27 J. FitzMaurice-Kelly *Historia de la literatura española* (Madrid: Librería Victoriano Suárez 1913) 243
28 Angel Custodio Vega 'Fray Luis de León' in *Historia general de las literaturas hispánicas*, edited by Guillermo Díaz-Plaja, vol. 2 (Barcelona: Editorial Barna 1951) 667
29 Manuel de Montoliú *Manual de historia de la literatura* 6th ed., vol. 1 (Barcelona: Editorial Cervantes 1957) 324–5
30 Ibid., 325

31 Agustín del Campo ' "Plurimembración y correlación" en Francisco de la Torre' *RFE* 30 (1946): 385–92
32 Dámaso Alonso 'Manierismos por reiteración, en Francisco de la Torre' *Strenae* (Salamanca: Universidad de Salamanca 1962) 36
33 Sena *Francisco de la Torre*, 7
34 Ibid., 127, fn. 114 (*sic*)

CHAPTER I

Poems and other material for which references are given in the text are from *Poesías*. See n.1 for the Introduction.

1 See, for example, Leone Ebreo *Dialoghi d'amore*, edited by Santino Caramello (Bari: Laterza 1929) 52–5, and Baldassare Castiglione *Il cortegiano*, edited by Vittorio Cian, 4th ed. rev. (Florence: Sansoni 1947) 392–4.
2 R.V. Merrill 'Platonism in Petrarch's *Canzoniere*' *MPh* 27 (1929): 161–74; and M.J. Woods 'Rhetoric in Garcilaso's First Eclogue' *MLN* 84 (1969): 143–56
3 Jorge de Sena *Francisco de la Torre e D. João de Almeida* (Paris: Centro Cultural Português 1974) 94–127
4 Boscán, in his 'Octava rima,' does postulate some ideas on love that fall within the Neo-Platonic framework. See Juan Boscán Almogáver *Obras poéticas* edited by Martín de Riquer, Antonio Comas, and Joaquín Molas (Barcelona: Universidad de Barcelona 1957), ll. 529–66. The fine arguments between love and desire, much debated by the Neo-Platonists, are briefly expounded by Cetina, his mysterious friend, Vadillo, and Pedro Laynez. See Gutierre de Cetina *Obras*, edited by Joaquín Hazañas y la Rúa, vol. 1 (Seville 1895, reprinted Mexico: Porrúa 1977), Sonnet 186, 166–7. Vadillo's verse is appended to that of Cetina; see *Obras*, vol. 2: 243–72. For Laynez, see Pedro Laynez *Obras*, edited by Joaquín de Entrambasaguas, vol. 2 (Madrid: CSIC 1951) 124–9. Two sonnets by Francisco de Aldana demonstrate the differences between Platonic and sensual love. See his *Poesías*, edited by Elias Rivers (Madrid: Espasa-Calpe 1957), Sonnets 12 and 37. An analysis of them may be read in Otis Green *Spain and the Western Tradition* vol. 1 (Madison: University of Wisconsin Press 1963), 134.
5 Sena *Francisco de la Torre* 107, n. 121
6 Ibid., 108
7 Ibid., 105–9
8 The sonnet proceeds from the Italian G. Amaltheo ('La viva neve e le vermiglie rose'). See J. Fucilla *Estudios sobre petrarquismo en España* (Madrid:

CSIC 1960) 141. Cf. Elicio's song in Cervantes's *La Galatea*, edited by J.B. Avalle-Arce, vol. 1 (Madrid: Espasa-Calpe 1968) 26.

9 The image does not appear to have had much attraction for Boscán and Garcilaso. An echo of it is to be found in Boscán's *epístola* to Diego Hurtado de Mendoza, and Garcilaso refers to it once in his first *canción*. Boscán's *epístola* may be found in Diego Hurtado de Mendoza's *Obras poéticas*, edited by William I. Knapp (Madrid: Miguel Ginesta 1877) 357. For Garcilaso, see Garcilaso de la Vega *Poesías castellanas completas*, edited by Elias Rivers (Madrid: Castalia 1969), Canción 1, ll. 17–19. Later poets, beginning with Cetina, use the image more frequently. For a theoretical explanation, see Fernando de Herrera's *Anotaciones* to Garcilaso's poetry in *Garcilaso de la Vega y sus comentaristas*, edited by Antonio Gallego Morell (Granada: Universidad de Granada 1966) 313.

10 Otis Green 'Courtly Love in the Spanish Cancioneros' *PMLA* 64 (1949): 301

11 In Herrera *Garcilaso de la Vega*, 305

12 I have not attempted to separate the courtly and Petrarchan aspects because of their close relationship. Nevertheless one should recognize that there are some elements more evidently of Petrarchan than of *cancionero* (or courtly) provenance: for example, the analysis of the poet's inner condition with a more acute awareness of the natural world in relation to his feelings; the contrast between past joy and present sorrow and a more sensitive use of colour; and the firmer establishment of the description of the lady – no longer the married, anonymous 'senhal' of Provençal tradition. Certain imagery, too, finds its source in Petrarch: the violent fire-ice and war-peace antitheses, the lady's features conceived metaphorically as, for example, gold, stars, pearls, ivory, roses. She is also the light of the poet's life, his guiding star, the sun, metaphors that give rise also to corollary images of clouds and storms. She is the sweet enemy who attracts her poet like a moth. But other imagery and ideas expressed by Petrarch are also to be found in *cancionero* verse; the war of love, the prisoner, the besieged eyes, the eyes as responsible for the poet's state and for opening the way to his heart, the arrows of love, the poet's blindness and bewilderment, the enumerated descriptions of love, the concept of love as a service that ennobles the lover, requests for mercy, descriptions of the suffering, the pleasure felt in suffering, the struggle between reason and desire, the distress in the presence of the lady.

13 Cf. also the contrast between Sonnet 23/II (already discussed) and Sonnet 26/I. Like the former, Sonnet 26/I contains courtly-Petrarchan imagery and Neo-Platonic phraseology, but the message clearly points to courtly triumph:

Las peligrosas brauas ondas de oro
donde perdió mi nauezilla el cielo,
el resplandor del soberano velo,
que esconde la deidad del alto coro;
    el estrellado y celestial tesoro
del florecido, aljofarado suelo;
la pertinacia y el dañado celo
del alma idolatrada que yo adoro;
    las iris de mi cielo sossegado;
la mansedumbre y el semblante humano
de quien agora libremente triunfo;
    el altiuo desdén del pecho elado,
armas fueron del crudo amor tirano
y agora son trofeos de mi triunfo.

14 The 'capital y caríssimo enemigo' referred to in these lines in all probability
    alludes to the beloved. Cf. Sonnet 10/1, line 5, 'al enemigo vencedor amado.'
    The use of the masculine term 'enemigo' reinforces the courtly-Petrarchan
    aspect, although the more normal expression in Golden Age verse was
    'dueño' (recalling the cruel or all-powerful *midons* of Provençal origin).
    Torre's image of 'enemigo' increases the tension of love by means of a vio-
    lent oxymoron, underlined by the superlative 'caríssimo.'

15 Cited in J.D. Passavant *Raphael d'Urbin et son père Giovani Santi*, translated
    by Jules Lunteschutz, vol. 1 (Paris: 1860) 501–2.

16 See R. Foulché-Delbosc 'Poésies inédites de Francisco de Figueroa' *RHi*
    25 (1911): 341–4. Cf. Gregorio Silvestre's description in his 'Visita de amor'
    Poesías, edited by A. Marín Ocete (Granada: Universidad de Granada
    1939) 138, and the very prosaic portrait by Jorge de Montemayor in Eclogue
    1 of *El Cancionero*, edited by Angel González Palencia (Madrid: Espasa-
    Calpe 1932). Herrera comments on the verbal portrait in *Garcilaso de la
    Vega*, 345. For a detailed study of the verbal portrait, see Gareth Davies
    'Pintura: Background and Sketch of a Seventeenth-Century Court Genre'
    Journal of the Warburg and Courtauld Institutes 38 (1975): 288–313.

17 In R. Menéndez Pidal 'Observaciones sobre las poesías de Francisco de
    Figueroa' *BRAE* 2 (1915): 469. Cf. L. Barahona de Soto, in Francisco
    Rodríguez Marín, ed., *Luis Barahona de Soto* (Madrid: Real Academia Espa-
    ñola 1903) 323–4 and 752.

18 Sena *Francisco de la Torre* 101

19 The 1631 edition of the Biblioteca Nacional shows an accent on 'Huyo' (thus
    'Huyó'), which I have followed. Nevertheless, the interpretation does not

differ radically. The poet's desire to flee the 'fuego deshonrado' is susbstantiated by his soul's shame at the action of the 'pensamiento altiuo.'

20 Sena *Francisco de la Torre* 11 and 105–27

21 Ibid., 125

22 Ibid., 106

23 For a history of the images in Spain, see María Rosa Lida de Malkiel 'Transmisión y recreación de temas grecolatinos' *RFH* 1 (1940): 21–63. Two other good studies are those of Peter Demetz 'The Elm and the Vine; Notes toward the History of a Marriage Topos' *PMLA* 73 (1958): 521–32, and George E. Erdman, Jr. 'Arboreal Figures in the Golden Age Sonnet' *PMLA* 84 (1969): 587–95.

24 Sena *Francisco de la Torre* 117

25 This idea is not dissimilar to the image of the transformation of the lover. For a good example of the death of the lover see Figueroa's *Canción*, '¡Ay débil corazón! ¡Ay flaca mano!' in Menéndez Pidal 'Observaciones' 314–16. The forlorn Tirsi laments: 'Que no soy Tirsi ya, aquel Tirsi vivo; / ... / allá en mi Fili vivo; en Tirsi muero.' Cf. also Herrera's 'Egloga venatoria,' with its much stronger eroticism:

> ¡Ah, cuántas veces entre aqueste juego
> a tu cuello los braços rodeara,
> i, en tus ojos mis ojos encendiendo,
> cuando mas descuidada de mi fuego,
> a tu boca el espíritu hurtara,
> mi espíritu en el tuyo convirtiendo,
> dulcemente muriendo.   (Fernando de Herrera *Poesías*, edited by Vicente García de Diego [Madrid: Espasa-Calpe 1962], ll. 2610–16).

26 Sena *Francisco de la Torre* 117

27 Cf., for example, Diego Hurtado de Mendoza's description of Adonis and Venus, seated on the grass:

> ... Trabándose estrecho con los brazos,
> la yerba y a sí mesmos apretaron,
> mezclando las palabras con abrazos;
> nunca revueltas vides rodearon
> el álamo con tantos embarazos,
> ni la verde y entretejida hiedra
> se pegó tanto al árbol o a la piedra.   (*Obras poéticas*, 244)

Or Aldana:

> ¿Cuál es la causa, mi Damón, que estando
> en la lucha de amor juntos trabados

con lenguas, brazos, pies y encadenados
cual vid que entre el jazmín se va enredando.   (Poesías, Sonnet 12)
Silvestre is equally erotic:
Y de allí del mismo amor mío encendida
con sus hermosos labios bebe y toca
el aire más caliente de mi boca,
haciendo de dos almas una vida.
Y un alma de dos cuerpos moradora
y dos cuerpos en uno más trabados
que jamás hiedra estuvo a olmo alguno.   (Poesías: Sonnet, 'Habiendo
sido ya más combatida' 248)

CHAPTER 2

1 See Doris Lessig *Ursprung und Entwicklung der Spanischen Ekloge bis 1650* (Geneva: Librairie Droz 1962) 177–216, for a list of poets who compose eclogues and the number of eclogues they produced.
2 The title, 'Bucólica del Tajo,' is rather unusual, since the banks of the Tagus serve as a setting for only three of the eclogues (1, 5, and 8). Eclogue 4 opens on the banks of the Tesín, a tributary of the Po, and Eclogue 6 on those of the Betis (Guadalquivir). Eclogues 2, 3, and 7 contain no references to specific rivers.
3 Lessig *Ursprung und Entwicklung* 149
4 Margot Arce de Vázquez *Garcilaso de la Vega* 2d ed. (Río Piedras: Universidad de Puerto Rico 1961) 103
5 Manuel José Quintana, ed. *Poesías selectas castellanas* (Madrid: Fuentenebros y Compañía 1807) xli
6 Quintana includes only one eclogue (the fourth) in his anthology, and appears to have overlooked the numerous storm references in the odes.
7 Angel Custodio Vega 'Fray Luis de León' in *Historia general de las literaturas hispánicas*, edited by Guillermo Díaz-Plaja, vol. 2 (Barcelona: Editorial Barna 1951) 667
8 Segundo Serrano Poncela *Formas de vida hispánica* (Madrid: Gredos 1963) 37
9 Dámaso Alonso, Agustín del Campo, and Jorge de Sena have analysed aspects of Torre's poetry but make no comment on the role of nature since it did not fall within the scope of their investigation. See Dámaso Alonso, 'Manierismos por reiteración en Francisco de la Torre' *Strenae* (Salamanca: Universidad de Salamanca 1962) 31–6; A. del Campo '"Plurimembración y correlación" en Francisco de la Torre' *RFE* 30: 385–92; and J. de Sena *Francisco de la Torre e D. João de Almeida* (Paris: Centro Cultural Português 1974).

10 Virgil, Ovid, and Claudian had used it. See D.A. Pearsall and E. Slater, *Landscapes and Seasons of the Medieval World* (Toronto: University of Toronto Press 1973) 6, 11, 21.

11 The classical references are common also in the background of the other eclogues (except the third, which has no introductory landscape).

12 See R. Menéndez Pidal 'Observaciones sobre las poesías de Francisco de Figueroa' *BRAE* 2 (1915): 321–3. Adverbs, such as 'de allí,' 'allende,' and 'más baxo,' the reference to 'pueblo,' and the non-pastoral name 'Ana Florisia,' indicate the realistic basis of Figueroa's description. The background of Montemayor's eclogue recalls the landscape in the seventh book of his novel *La Diana*. Changes of perspective, together with adverbial expressions, such as 'allí,' 'de la otra parte,' 'a gran trecho de allí,' and 'de la una parte,' point to the realistic orientations of his description. See Jorge de Montemayor *El cancionero*, edited by Angel González Palencia (Madrid: Espasa-Calpe 1932) 74–89.

13 Thanks perhaps to Virgil, there is a danger of equating Arcadia with the *locus ameonus*. Certainly the Latin poet did not dwell on the mountainous aspect of his far-away ideal but associated it rather with Pan, the god of herdsmen and inventor of the panpipe. Sannazaro's Arcadia, however, expands on the Virgilian model to include lofty mountains and towering cliffs (for example, *Prosa* 1, 5, and 8). In one notable instance – the description of the stream Erymanthus in *Prosa* 5 – the violence of the water creates a boiling white foam which bursts out at the foot of the mountain onto a plain: 'Nè guari oltra a duo milia passi andati fummo, che al capo d'un fiume chiamato Erimanto pervenimmo; il quale da pie' d'un monte per una rottura di pietra viva con un rumore grandissimo e spaventevole, e con certi bollori di bianche schiume si caccia fore nel piano e per quello transcorrendo, col suo mormorio va fatigando le vivine selve.' (*Opere*, edited by Enrico Carrara [Turin: Editrice Torinese 1952] 88–9). Despite a vague similarity in the rapid movement of water and a sense of movement from mountains to plains, there is no indication of any direct debt on Torre's part.

14 From the following list it is evident that, at least in the Spanish pastoral, the pattern does not appear to have been rigorously kept. Nevertheless, it will also be seen that none of the poets begins his eclogues with an evening scene as consistently as Torre, or indeed so consistently provides a temporal framework for the 'action':

	Poem begins	*Poem ends*
FRANCISCO DE LA TORRE		
Eclogue 1	dawn	midday
Eclogue 2	evening [changes to dawn, stanza 16]	?

Eclogue 3	?	?
Eclogue 4	evening	night
Eclogue 5	evening [changes to dawn, stanza 17]	?
Eclogue 6	evening	dawn
Eclogue 7	evening	?
Eclogue 8	dawn	evening
HERNANDO DE ACUÑA		
Eclogue 1	dawn	?
Eclogue 2	?	?
LUIS BARAHONA DE SOTO		
Eclogue 1	?	night
Eclogue 2	?	?
Eclogue 3	?	?
Eclogue 4	?	?
Eclogue 5	?	?
FRANCISCO DE FIGUEROA		
'Egloga pastoral'	?	?
Eclogue: 'Del Betis a la orilla'	?	?
GARCILASO DE LA VEGA		
Eclogue 1	dawn	evening
Eclogue 2	?	dawn
Eclogue 3	midday	evening
FERNANDO DE HERRERA		
Egloga venatoria (*Poesías*)	?	?
Eclogue 1 (*Rimas inéditas*)	?	?
Eclogue 2 ” ”	?	?
Eclogue 3 ” ”	?	?
Eclogue 4 ” ”	dawn	?
DIEGO HURTADO DE MENDOZA		
Eclogue 1	midday	?
Eclogue 2	?	?
Eclogue 3	?	?
PEDRO LAYNEZ		
Eclogue 1	midday	?
Eclogue 2	?	?
Eclogue 3	afternoon	evening
JORGE DE MONTEMAYOR		
Eclogue 1	?	evening
Eclogue 2	?	evening

Eclogue 3   ?   evening

Eclogue 4   ?   evening

15 José María de Cossío *Fábulas mitológicas en España* (Madrid: Espasa-Calpe 1952) 215

16 Joseph Gillet *Propalladia and Other Works of Bartolomé de Torres Naharro*, transcribed, edited, and completed by Otis H. Green, vol. 4 (Philadelphia: University of Pennsylvania Press 1961) 265

17 It is significant that in pastoral poetry, even when there is dialogue, the participants often do not commiserate directly with each other but seek attention or compassion from nature. The result is that the dialogues are, in effect, parallel monologues.

18 See, for example, 'El árbol caído' in J. Meléndez Valdés *Poesías*, edited by Pedro Salinas (Madrid: Espasa-Calpe 1925) 191–4.

19 The intimate address normally consists of appeals made by poets to objects of nature (for example, trees, animals) for the latter to assist them or to participate with them in their sorrow. Such is the use observed by María Rosa Lida de Malkiel in her article 'Transmisión y recreación de temas grecolations' *RFH* 1 (1940): 21–63. It is of interest to note that in this article, the only poets (besides Francisco de la Torre) who use the second-person address belong to the final quarter of the sixteenth century (Herrera) or to the seventeenth and eighteenth centuries.

20 A similar observation was made by R.M. MacAndrew. See his *Naturalism in Spanish Poetry from the Origins to 1900* (Aberdeen: Milne & Hutchinson 1931) 37. Cf. also M.J. Woods *The Poet and the Natural World in the Age of Góngora* (Oxford: Oxford University Press 1978) 61. Note the comment by Woods that before the end of the sixteenth century it was not easy to find examples of poems where an object of nature became the focus of attention. Torre's *canciones* do not praise nature or its creatures, but the poet's attitude is one of sympathy and understanding. For Rioja's work, consult *Poetas líricos de los siglos xvi y xvii*, edited by Adolfo del Castro, vol. 32, part 1 (Madrid: BAE 1854) 375–89.

21 Alonso Zamora Vicente *De Garcilaso a Valle-Inclán* (Buenos Aires: Editorial Sudamericana 1950) 75

CHAPTER 3

1 Dámaso Alonso 'Manierismos por reiteración, en Francisco de la Torre' *Strenae* (Salamanca: Universidad de Salamanca 1962) 36

2 W. Pabst *La creación gongorina en los poemas 'Polifemo' y 'Soledades'*, translated by Nicolás Marín (Madrid: CSIC 1966) 35

3 Dámaso Alonso *Estudios y ensayos gongorinos* 2d ed. (Madrid: Gredos 1960) 166

4 See Juan de Mena *El laberinto de Fortuna*, edited by José Manuel Blecua (Madrid: Espasa-Calpe 1960) lxxxiii. See also María Rosa Lida de Malkiel *Juan de Mena* (Mexico: Nueva Revista de Filología Hispánica 1950) 203–5.

5 Dámaso Alonso *Estudios* 152

6 The percentage frequency of *bimembres* in Torre's and Figueroa's verse may not appear statistically remarkable. The most complete edition of Francisco de Figueroa's verse *Poesías*, is that of Ángel González Palencia (Madrid, 1943), which contains some 5,462 lines. The total number of *bimembres* is approximately fifty, or 0.92 per 100 lines. Torre composed some 4,774 lines, of which approximately 125 are *bimembres*, or 2.61 per 100 lines. We should keep in mind, before dismissing these percentages as insignificant, that the percentage basis is calculated on *all* lines of poetry, including, in the case of Torre, numerous poems (ten *endechas* and two odes, totalling 644 lines) written entirely in hexasyllabic or heptasyllabic lines. (Nevertheless, even in these poems the frequent occurrence of epanalepsis between two lines – with the resulting effect of counterbalance – echoes Torre's interest in the technique of bifurcation, e.g., 'o llore de contino, / o nunca el alma llore,' Ode 6/1; 'Tú fuiste querida, / y oluidada fuiste,' Endecha 6, ll. 9–10; 'Llorando me dejas, / hallasme llorando,' Endecha 9, ll. 61–2.) What we should also bear in mind is the marked infrequency of *bimembres* in poets preceding Torre, e.g., Garcilaso, Boscán, Acuña, Diego Hurtado de Mendoza.

7 A rapid calculation shows some fifty-five examples in Eclogues 1 and 5, and approximately thirty-two in the remaining six.

8 Wolfgang Kayser *Interpretación y análisis de la obra literaria* 4th ed. rev. (Madrid: Gredos 1961) 156

9 See Dámaso Alonso *Vida y obra de Medrano* vol. 1 (Madrid: CSIC 1948) 146–7. A similar controlling effect of the emotions may be seen also in Eclogue 2, stanza 9 and Eclogue 7, stanza 4.

10 Pedro Espinosa is another poet who comes to mind as an exponent of the *bimembre* and parallelism. Some of his early poems, especially, are heavily dependent on the complicated interplay of the devices. See, for example, poems 4, 12, 23, 24, 26, 27, and 30 in *Poesías completas*, edited by Francisco López Estrada (Madrid: Espasa-Calpe 1975).

11 Dámaso Alonso 'Manierismos por reiteración' 31–6

12 This example also constitutes anadiplosis (the repetition of a word, or words, ending a line at the beginning of the following line). Other examples in Torre can be found in Eclogue 1, stanza 16, and Eclogue 3, ll. 106–7.

13 Garcilaso uses the mannerism twice. See *Poesías castellanas completas*, edited
by Elias Rivers. Madrid: Castalia 1969:
¡Mi prendedero d'oro, si es perdido!
¡Oh cuitada de mí, mi prendedero!   (Eclogue 2, ll. 850–1)
Guardarme como en los pasados años
D'otros graves peligros me guardaron.   (Canción 4, ll. 25–6)
Diego Hurtado de Mendoza and Hernando de Acuña each use epanalep-
sis once. See respectively Diego Hurtado de Mendoza *Obras poéticas*, edited
by William I. Knapp (Madrid: Miguel Ginasta 1877), Eclogue 2: 'Sospiro
yo, responde él y sospira' (p. 69); and Hernando de Acuña *Varias poesías*,
edited by Elena Catena de Vindel (Madrid: CSIC 1954), 'Canto de Silvano':
'Al ayre essos cabellos vi esparcirse / en mil nudos al ayre essos cabellos.'
Fray Luis de León connects stanzas 16 and 17 of his famous poem, 'Vida
retirada,' with the device: 'Tendido yo a la sombra, esté cantando. / A la
sombra tendido / ...' See *The Original Poems*, edited by Edward Sarmiento.
(Manchester: Manchester University Press, 1953) 8. Pedro Laynez employs
epanalepsis a little more frequently. See *Obras*, edited by Joaquín de En-
trambasaguas, vol. 2 (Madrid: CSIC 1951):
Ablanda un poco el duro pecho, ablanda   (Eclogue 1, p. 59)
Dezir también que es cruda Galatea
bien claro la ocasión dellas lo dize   (Eclogue 1, p. 64)
Todo por sí da muerte, y junto todo   (Eclogue 1, p. 67)
Señora de mi alma y de mi vida,
y de mi voluntad siempre Señora.   (Eclogue 3, p. 93)
Haziendo en la vida lo que en muerte hizo   (Eclogue 3, p. 99)
Francisco de Medrano too is not unacquainted with the device. See, for
example, *Vida y obra de Medrano* 2:
Venciome, y tan dichoso fue vencido.   (Sonnet 5)
Los primores de el cielo, los primores   (Sonnet 37)
Tanto valor encierra y saber tanto   (Sonnet 49)
Más ligero que el gamo, y que el neboso
Aquilón, más ligero.   (Ode 24)
Vimosla ya, Leucido, ya la vimos   (Ode 25)
Medrano also employs a more complicated form of epanalepsis. The initial
word of a line is not repeated at the end of the same line or the following,
but at the beginning of a succeeding line. This cannot, however, be con-
sidered anaphora, for the repeated word clearly returns to, and counter-
balances, the model. For example:
Dejará Eutropo sus preciosos lares,
sus rentas, sus lugares,
y quanto le evanece

dejará: ...   (Ode 2, stanza 4)
Ardenme aquellos ojos
negros de la Amarilis que, serenos,
roban el sol; aquellos sus enojos
árdenme ...   (Ode 12, stanza 4)
Oyó el cielo mi voto, Elisa, el cielo
lo oyó, Elisa ...   (Ode 25, stanza 1)

Dámaso Alonso and Reckert have seen in these examples a classical
influence, notably that of Horace.

14 For a number of examples from classical writers, consult Abraham Fraunce's
    interesting work *The Arcadian Rhetorike*, edited from the edition of 1588
    (Oxford: Oxford University Press 1950) 45 and 60. Fraunce's interests
    were wide, and he frequently refers with admiration to Garcilaso. Curiously,
    too, one of his examples of epanalepsis is taken from Boscán: 'Contem-
    plando tras esto en las mudanças, / De la mar, y d'el viento contem-
    plando' (p. 46). See also K.L. Selig's article 'Garcilaso in Sixteenth-Century
    England' *RF* 84 (1972): 368–71. Further examples of epanalepsis in classical
    writers may be found in Peter Dronke *Medieval Latin and the Rise of the
    European Love-Lyric* vol. 1 (Oxford: Oxford University Press 1965) 177 and
    257.
15 Agustín del Campo '"Plurimembración y correlación" en Francisco de la
    Torre' *RFE* 30 (1946): 385–6; Dámaso Alonso 'Manierismos por reitera-
    ción' 35
16 Dámaso Alonso 'Manierismos por reiteración' 35
17 Dámaso Alonso *Poesía española* 4th ed. (Madrid: Gredos 1962) 438
18 See the Zamora Vicente edition of Francisco de la Torre's *Poesías* (Madrid:
    Espasa-Calpe 1956) 45, note to line 10.
19 Other examples are Sonnet 22/1; Eclogue 1, stanzas 32 and 39.
20 Manuel José Quintana, ed. *Poesías selectas castellanas* (Madrid: Fuentene-
    bros y Compañía 1807) xli
21 Malkiel *Juan de Mena* 317
22 In Luis de Góngora *Las Soledades*, edited by Dámaso Alonso (Madrid:
    Sociedad de Estudios y Publicaciones 1956) 30. Cf. the comments made
    recently by M.J. Woods that extended introductory descriptions were not
    infrequent in Baroque poets, and that such descriptions went beyond the
    preparatory function practised by Renaissance poets. The intention was to
    present nature 'in a surprising way, rather than merely factually.' Woods
    then quotes from a pastoral poem by Pedro de Godoy 'which is unremark-
    able save for its opening description of the riverside scene, which lasts some
    fifty lines, and in which there is such a welter of subordinate adverbial
    clauses as detail is added to detail that the reader begins to wonder if he will

ever reach the main verb.' See *The Poet and the Natural World in the Age of Góngora* (Oxford: Oxford University Press 1978) 51–2. Certainly Torre's descriptions do not contain such a wealth of natural fruits, more in keeping with the cornucopia theme advanced later by Woods. Nevertheless, what matters here is the question of technique, and in that Torre shows surprising affinity with seventeenth-century poets.

23 Cf. Malkiel's comment regarding Juan de Mena's use of the relative: 'Incomoda a la percepción moderna de estilo poético la extraña predilección del *Laberinto* por los relativos ... que hoy resultan pedantes y prosaicos ... Asimismo presta colorido latino el relativo que introduce una oración ...' (*Juan de Mena* 299). A little later (p. 300) she adds: 'No es raro en Mena el uso de "cuyo" ... Góngora y sus secuaces usan también este relativo, con frecuencia chocante para nosotros.'

24 Other examples include the negative anaphora in Eclogue 1, stanzas 31 and 32; anaphoric 'si' in stanzas 26 and 28 of Eclogue 1; 'pues ...tú sola,' Eclogue 2, stanzas 7 and 8; 'quando,' Endecha 8, ll. 57, 61, 65.

25 Margot Arce de Vázquez *Garcilaso de la Vega* 2d ed. (Río Piedras: Universidad de Puerto Rico, 1961) 129

26 María Rosa Lida de Malkiel 'Transmisión y recreación de temas grecolatinos en la poesía lírica española' *RFH* 1 (1940): 52

27 Eduardo Sarmiento *Concordancia de las obras poéticas en castellano de Garcilaso de la Vega* (Madrid: Castalia 1970) 574

28 The difference in procedure between Torre and Garcilaso and his contemporaries is reflected to some degree in a comparison of Torre's Canción 3/II and Hurtado de Mendoza's *canción*, 'Ya el sol revuelve con dorado freno' (*Obras poéticas*, 38–40). Both poems are based on Petrarch's *canzone*, 'Ne la stagion che 'l ciel rapido inchina.' Although Torre follows Petrarch more closely in his development of the poem, he differs from both his model and Mendoza in his use of mythological figures. Mendoza's poem does not contain a single mythological reference, whereas Torre's version opens with a picture of Phoebus descending, not into the sea, but into the 'concha espaciosa' of Glaucus and Thetis. In the second stanza Phoebus is replaced by Apollo, and in stanza 4 the secure, but exhausted sailor meditates in mythological terms on the storm from which he has escaped: 'Quantas vezes vio a Iúputer triunfante, / quantas en su dolor piadoso y blando.' Finally, in stanza 5, the sunset is again portrayed as the end of Phoebus's journey across the sky.

29 For an explanation, see Peter Demetz 'The Elm and the Vine. Notes toward the History of a Marriage Topos' *PMLA* 73 (1958): 521–32. See also Antonio Vilanova *Las fuentes del Polifemo* vol. 2 (Madrid: CSIC 1957) 422. For a

treatment of arboreal imagery in Golden Age poetry, see E. George Erdman, Jr. 'Arboreal Figures in the Golden Age Sonnet' *PMLA* 84 (1969): 587–95.

30 See Malkiel 'Transmisión y recreación,' 31–52.

31 See Dámaso Alonso *La lengua poética de Góngora* 3d. ed. corrected (Madrid: CSIC 1961) 77–9; Antonio Vilanova *Las fuentes del Polifemo* vol. 2, 809–72, and David Kossoff *Vocabulario de la obra poética de Herrera* (Madrid: Real Academia Española 1966) ix–xiv.

32 Margherita Morreale *Castiglione y Boscán: el ideal cortesano en el renacimiento español* vol. 1 (Madrid: Real Academia Española 1959) 93

33 Ramón Menéndez Pidal *Manual de gramática histórica española* 11th ed. (Madrid: Espasa-Calpe 1962) 221

34 Dámaso Alonso *Góngora y el Polifemo* 4th ed., vol. 1 (Madrid: Gredos 1963) 130. Of interest also is that the more vehement and emotionally expressive verse of Herrera contains relatively few 'esdrújulos.' Cf. Fernando de Herrera *Rimas inéditas*, edited by José Manuel Blecua (Madrid: CSIC 1948) 17: 'Herrera no utilizó con mucha frecuencia los esdrújulos ...'

35 Fernando de Herrera *Anotaciones* in *Garcilaso de la Vega y sus comentaristas*, edited by Antonio Gallego Morell (Granada, Universidad de Granada 1966) 291

36 Dámaso Alonso *Vida y obra de Medrano* vol. 1, 172

37 Ibid., 173

38 Dámaso Alonso and Reckert draw attention to the use of the single verb with plural subject as being a 'Latinismo frecuente' in Medrano's poetry. See Dámaso Alonso and Stephen Reckert, *Vida y obra de Medrano*, vol. 2 (Madrid: CSIC 1958) 133, note to ll. 30–2.

39 For a review of *tmesis*, see G.L. Stagg, 'Tmesis in the Verse of Fray Luis de León and Others: a Western Romance Mannerism,' in *Linguistics and Literary Studies in Honor of Helmut A. Hatzfeld* (Washington: Catholic University of America Press 1964) 385–92.

40 For a discussion of the controversy surrounding 'hierba' and 'vista,' see E. Rivers 'On the Text of Garcilaso' *HR* 42 (1974): 43–9. The line 'la vista y el oído deleitando' does occur in the disputed 'Fábula de Narciso,' attributed to both Figueroa and Silvestre. See Figueroa *Poesías*, stanza 32; and Gregorio Silvestre *Poesías*, edited by A. Marín Ocete (Granada: Universidad de Granada 1939).

41 Arce de Vázquez *Garcilaso de la Vega*, 105

42 See Edith Rogers's article on colour in Golden Age verse: 'El color en la poesía española del renacimiento y del barroco' *RFE* 47 (1964): 247.

43 Dámaso Alonso *Poesía española* 129

44 Rudolph Baehr *Manual de versificación española*, translated and adapted by K. Wagner and F. López Estrada (Madrid: Gredos 1970) 362

45 Marcelino Menéndez y Pelayo *Horacio en España* vol. 2 (Madrid: Dubrull 1885) 38
46 Baehr, 363 and 370
47 Tomás Navarro Tomás *Métrica española* (New York: Compañía General de Ediciones 1966) 210. Both Navarro and Baehr (p. 100) overlook Ode 5/I.
48 See Menéndez y Pelayo *Horacio* vol. 2, 43–8.
49 In view of this remarkable consistency, the attribution to Torre of two sonnets 'El que de hidropesía está doliente' and 'Quiero contar, Fileno, mi cuidado' (J. de Sena, *Francisco de la Torre e D. João de Almeida* (Paris: Centro Cultural Português 1974) 308–9) may be questioned, since the paradigms in the sestets are respectively CDC : DCD and CDD : CEE (or CDDC : EE). (It should be pointed out that Sena is well aware of this discrepancy of rhyme-pattern. See ibid., 153 and 171.)
50 My reading suggests a somewhat different paradigm in Canciones 2/I and I and 4/II than those offered by Sena, ibid., 111. In his opinion Canción 2/I and 4/II are identical (abcabc : cdeeDFF with a commiato, or closing strophe, AbB), whereas Canción 1/II differs slightly (abcabc : cdecDFF : AbB). According to my reading all three *canciones* have an identical paradigm (based on Petrarch's famous 'Chiare, fresche e dolci acque'): abc abc : cdeeDFF : AbB.
51 Dámaso Alonso *Poesía española* 75
52 Dámaso Alonso *Estudios ... gongorinos* 204

CONCLUSION

1 Baltasar Gracián *Agudeza y arte de ingenio*, edited by E. Correa Calderón, vol. 1 (Madrid: Castalia 1969) 78
2 Stanzas 39 and 40 of Eclogue 1 echo to some degree the amoebean song of Garcilaso's third eclogue, although Crawford feels that they are a free imitation of the last part of Virgil's seventh eclogue. Apart from the similarity between Sonnet 22/I, 'Claro y sagrado Sol ...' and Herrera's 'Rojo sol que con llama gloriosa,' further Spanish influence is tenuous. The expression 'La noche sossegada' (Eclogue 6, stanza 28) recalls that of San Juan de la Cruz in his 'Cántico espiritual' (stanza 14), composed probably between 1578 and 1584. However, it already appears as 'sossegada noche' in Gil Polo's *Diana enamorada*, published 1564, and later in Jerónimo de Lomas Cantoral's verse (*Obras* [Madrid: Pierres Cosin 1578] fol. 414). Another line, Eclogue 4, stanza 12, line 7, 'al son dulce acordado,' also calls attention because it is identical to the penultimate line of Fray Luis de León's 'Vida retirada,' but there is no way, of course, of ascertaining which poem was written first.

3 Joseph G. Fucilla *Estudios sobre el petrarquismo en España* (Madrid: CSIC 1960) 139–43; Eugenio Mele 'Sobre canciones y sonetos italianos y españoles' *Revista castellana* 5 (1919): 209–22; J.P.W. Crawford 'Francisco de la Torre y sus poesías,' *Homenaje a Menéndez Pidal*, vol. 2 (Madrid: Hernando 1925) 431–46

4 J. FitzMaurice-Kelly *Historia de la literatura española* (Madrid: Librería Victoriano Suárez 1913), 243

5 Herrera, of course, frequently ascends to the heavens in pursuit of his lady – her poetic name, Luz, Estrella, Sol, underlines the celestial direction of his thought – but the relationship is essentially between the beloved and him, and there is no thought of seeing love as a force potentially existing between or binding other objects.

6 M.J. Woods *The Poet and the Natural World in the Age of Góngora* (Oxford: Oxford University Press 1978) 15

7 Stylistic dissimilarities are important also in determining the differences between Torre and one of the poets with whom he has been frequently identified, Juan de Almeida. There is, for example, a marked lack of *bimembres*, parallelism, the relative pronoun 'cuyo,' and not a single instance of epanalepsis in Almeida's verse. In addition, certain realistic and satiric traits that appear in Almeida's work (Sonnets VII, XVI, Lira I, Octavas III, in Sena's monograph) are not consonant with the tenor of Torre's poems.

Selected Bibliography

ABBREVIATIONS

BAE	Biblioteca de Autores Españoles
BBMP	*Boletín de la biblioteca Menéndez y Pelayo*
BHS	*Bulletin of Hispanic Studies*
BRAE	*Boletín de la Real Academia Española*
CA	*Cuadernos americanos*
CSIC	Consejo Superior de Investigaciones Científicas
HR	*Hispanic Review*
MLN	*Modern Language Notes*
MPh	*Modern Philology*
PMLA	*Publications of the Modern Language Association of America*
RF	*Romanische Forschungen*
RFE	*Revista de filología española*
RFH	*Revista de filología hispánica*
RHi	*Revue hispanique*

Acuña, Hernando de *Varias poesías*, edited by Elena Catena de Vindel. Madrid: CSIC 1954

Alborg, Juan Luis *Historia de la literatura española* 2 vols., 2d ed. Madrid: Gredos 1970

Aldana, Francisco de *Poesías*, edited by Elias Rivers. Madrid: Espasa-Calpe 1957

Alemany y Selfa, Bernardo *Vocabulario de las obras de don Luis de Góngora y Argote* Madrid: Real Academia Española 1930

Alonso, Dámaso *Estudios y ensayos gongorinos* 2d ed. Madrid: Gredos 1960

– *Góngora y el Polifemo* 2 vols. 4th ed. Madrid: Gredos 1961

- *La lengua poética de Góngora* 3d ed. corrected. Madrid: CSIC 1961
- 'Manierismos por reiteración, en Francisco de la Torre' *Strenae* Salamanca: Universidad de Salamanca 1962, 31–6
- *Poesía española* 4th ed. Madrid: Gredos 1962
- *Vida y obra de Medrano* vol. 1. Madrid: CSIC 1948
Alonso, Dámaso, and Bousoño, Carlos *Seis calas en la expresión literaria española* 2d ed. Madrid: Gredos 1963
Alonso, Dámaso, and Reckert, Stephen *Vida y obra de Medrano* vol. 2. Madrid: CSIC 1958
Alonso Cortés, Narciso 'Algunos datos sobre Hernando de Acuña y Francisco de la Torre' *HR* 9 (1941): 41–7
Alvar, Manuel 'Don Francisco de la Torre, amigo de Calderón' *RFE* 21 (1947): 155–61
Aparici, María Pilar 'Teorías amorosas en la lírica castellana del siglo XVI' *BBMP* 44 (1968): 121–67
Arce de Vázquez, Margot *Garcilaso de la Vega* 2d. ed. Río Piedras: Universidad de Puerto Rico 1961
Arjona, J.H. 'The Use of Autorhymes in the XVIIth Century "Comedia"' *HR* 21 (1953): 273–301
Artiles, Miguel *Paisaje y poesía en la Edad Media* La Laguna, Canary Is.: Universidad de La Laguna 1960
Asensio, Eugenio *Poética y realidad en el cancionero peninsular de la edad media* Madrid: Gredos 1957
Avalle-Arce, J.B. *La novela pastoril española* Madrid: Revista de Occidente 1959
Baehr, Rudolph *Manual de versificación española*, translated and adapted by K. Wagner and F. López Estrada. Madrid: Gredos 1970
Baker, Herschel *The Image of Man* New York: Harper & Row 1961
Balbín, Rafael de *Sistema de rítmica castellana* 2d ed. Madrid: Gredos 1968
Bataillon, Marcel 'La tortolica de "Fontefrida" y del "Cántico espiritual"' in *Varia lección de clásicos españoles* Madrid: Gredos 1964, 144–66
Bayo, Marcial José *Virgilio y la pastoral española del renacimiento 1480–1550* 2d ed. Madrid: Gredos 1970
Bianchini, Andreina 'Fernando de Herrera's *Anotaciones*: A New Look at His Sources and the Significance of His Poetics' *RF* 88 (1976): 27–42
Biblioteca de Autores Españoles vol. 16, edited by Agustín Durán, and vols. 42 and 71 edited by M. Rivadeneyra. Madrid: Publicidad 1851, Rivadeneyra 1857 and Aribau y Cía 1880
Blecua, José Manuel *Sobre poesía de la edad de oro* Madrid: Gredos 1970
- 'El poeta Francisco de la Torre Sevil, amigo de Gracián' *Mediterráneo* 6 (1944): 115–26

Boscán Almogáver, Juan *Obras poéticas*, edited by Martín de Riquer, Antonio Comas, Joaquín Molas. Barcelona: Universidad de Barcelona 1957

Bousoño, Carlos *Teoría de la expresión poética* 4th ed. Madrid: Gredos 1966

Campo, Agustín del '"Plurimembración y correlación" en Francisco de la Torre' *RFE* 30 (1946): 385–92

Carrara, Enrico 'La poesia pastorale' in *Storia dei generi letterari italiani* vol. 5. Milan: Editrice Vallarda, n.d.

Castiglione, Baldassare *Il cortegiano*, edited by Vittorio Cian. 4th ed. rev. Florence: Sansoni 1947

Castro, Adolfo del, ed. *Poetas líricos de los siglos* XVI y XVII, vol. 32, part 1. Madrid: BAE 1854

Cervantes, Miguel de *La Galatea*, edited by J.B. Avalle-Arce. 2 vols. Madrid: Espasa-Calpe 1968

Cetina, Gutierre de *Obras*, edited by Joaquín Hazañas y la Rúa. Seville 1895; reprinted Mexico: Porrúa 1977

Clark, Kenneth *Landscape into Art* London: Penguin 1961

Collard, Andrée *Nueva poesía: conceptismo, culteranismo en la crítica española* Waltham, Mass., and Madrid: Brandeis University and Castalia 1967

Correa, Gustavo 'Garcilaso y la mitología' *HR* 45 (1977): 269–81

Cossío, José María de *Fábulas mitológicas en España* Madrid: Espasa-Calpe 1952

Coster, Adolphe *Fernando de Herrera* Paris: Librairie Ancienne 1908

– 'Sur Francisco de la Torre' *RHi* 45 (1925): 74–132

Crawford, J.P.W. 'Francisco de la Torre and Juan de Almeida' *MLN* 42 (1927): 365–71

– 'Francisco de la Torre y sus poesías' *Homenaje a Menéndez Pidal* vol. 2. Madrid: Hernando 1925, 431–46

– 'Sources of an Eclogue of Francisco de la Torre' *MLN* 30 (1915): 214–15

Curtius, E.R. *European Literature and the Latin Middle Ages* translated by Willard Task. New York: Harper & Row 1963

Davies, Gareth 'Pintura: Background and Sketch of a Seventeenth-Century Court Genre' *Journal of the Warburg and Courtauld Institutes* 38 (1975): 288–313

Demetz, Peter 'The Elm and the Vine: Notes toward the History of a Marriage Topos' *PMLA* 73 (1958): 521–32

Díaz-Plaja, Guillermo, ed. *Historia general de la literaturas hispánicas* 6 vols. Barcelona: Editorial Barna 1951

Díaz Rengifo, J. *Arte poética española* Salamanca 1592; reprinted Madrid: Ministerio de Educación y Ciencias 1977

Díez Echarri, Emiliano *Teorías métricas del siglo de oro* 1948; reprinted Madrid: CSIC 1970

Dronke, Peter *Medieval Latin and the Rise of the European Love-Lyric* vol. 1. Oxford: Oxford University Press 1965

Ebreo, Leone *Dialoghi d'amore*, edited by Santino Caramella. Bari: Laterza 1929

Ellrodt, Robert *Neoplatonism in the Poetry of Spenser* Geneva: E. Droz 1960

Empson, William *Some Versions of the Pastoral* London: Chatto & Windus 1950

Entrambasaguas, Joaquín de. Review of Francisco de la Torre, *Poesías*, edited by A. Zamora Vicente, in *RFE* 28 (1944): 480–6

Erdman, E. George, Jr. 'Arboreal Figures in the Golden Age Sonnet' *PMLA* 54 (1969): 587–95

Espinosa, Pedro *Poesías completas*, edited by Francisco López Estrada. Madrid: Espasa-Calpe 1975

Faria y Sousa, Manuel, ed. *Lusiadas de Luis de Camoens* Lisbon: Imprenta Nacional-Casa da Moeda 1972

Fernández-Guerra y Orbe, Aureliano 'Francisco de la Torre' in *Discursos leídos ante la Real Academia Española* Madrid: Rivadeneyra 1857

Figueroa, Francisco de *Poesías*, edited by Angel González Palencia. Madrid: Sociedad de bibliófilos españoles 1943

– *Poesías*, edited by Luis Tribaldos de Toledo, in *Poesías de los Argensolas y Figueroa* Madrid: Imprenta Real 1804

FitzMaurice-Kelly, J. *Historia de la literatura española* Madrid: Librería Victoriano Suárez 1913

Forster, Leonard *The Icy Fire: Five Studies in European Petrarchism* Cambridge: Cambridge University Press 1969

Foulché-Delbosc, R. 'Poésies inédites de Francisco de Figueroa' *RHi* 25 (1911): 327–44

Fraunce, Abraham *The Arcadian Rhetoricke* edited from the edition of 1588. Oxford: Oxford University Press 1950

Fucilla, J. *Estudios sobre el petrarquismo en España* Madrid: CSIC 1960

– '"Parole identiche" in the Sonnet and Other Verse Forms' *PMLA* 50 (1935): 372–402

– 'Two Generations of Petrarchism and Petrarchists in Spain' *MPh* 27 (1929–1930): 277–95

Gállego, Julián *Visión y símbolos en la pintura española del Siglo de Oro* Madrid: Aguilar 1972

Gallego Morell, Antonio, ed. *Estudios sobre poesía española del primer siglo de oro* Madrid: Insula 1970

– *Garcilaso de la Vega y sus comentaristas* Granada: Universidad de Granada 1966

Garcilaso de la Vega *Obras*, edited by Tomás Navarro Tomás. Madrid: Espasa-Calpe 1958

– *Poesías castellanas completas*, edited by Elias Rivers. Madrid: Castalia 1969

Gerhardt, Mia I. *La pastorale: Essai d'analyse littéraire* Assen, Netherlands: Van Gorcum & Company 1950

Giamatti, A.B. *The Earthly Paradise and the Renaissance Epic* Princeton: Princeton University Press 1966

Gillet, Joseph *Propalladia and Other Works of Bartolomé de Torres Naharro* vol. 4, transcribed and edited and completed by Otis Green. Philadelphia: University of Pennsylvania Press 1961

Góngora, Luis de *Las Soledades*, edited by Dámaso Alonso. Madrid: Sociedad de Estudios y Publicaciones 1956

– *Obras completas*, edited by Juan and Isabel Millé y Giménez. Madrid: Aguilar 1956

– *Sonetos completos*, edited by Biruté Ciplijauskaite. Madrid: Castalia 1969

González de Escandón, Blanca *Los temas del 'Carpe diem' y la brevedad de la vida en la poesía* Barcelona: Universidad de Barcelona 1938

González López, Emilio *Historia de la literatura española* vol. 2. New York: Las Américas 1962

González Palencia, A., and Mele, Eugenio *Vida y obras de don Diego Hurtado de Mendoza* 3 vols. Madrid: Instituto de Valencia de San Juan 1943

Gracián, Baltasar *Agudeza y arte de ingenio* edited by E. Correa Calderón. 2 vols. Madrid: Castalia 1969

Green, Otis 'Courtly Love in the Spanish "Cancioneros"' *PMLA* 64 (1949): 247–301

– *El amor cortés en Quevedo* Saragossa: Librería General 1955

– *Spain and the Western Tradition* 4 vols. Madison: University of Wisconsin Press 1963–1967

Greg, W.W. *Pastoral Poetry and Pastoral Drama* London: A.H. Bullen 1906

Guillén, Jorge *Lenguaje y poesía* Madrid: Alianza 1969

Hatzfeld, Helmut *Estudios sobre el barroco* 2d ed. Madrid: Gredos 1966

Henríquez Ureña, Pedro *Estudios de versificación española* Buenos Aires: Universidad de Buenos Aires 1961

Herrera, Fernando de *Poesías*, edited by Vicente García de Diego. Madrid: Espasa-Calpe 1962

– *Rimas inéditas*, edited by José Manuel Blecua. Madrid: CSIC 1948

Horatius Flaccus *Odes and Epodes*, edited by P. Shorey; revised by P. Shorey and G.J. Laing. Chicago: Benj. H. Sanborn & Co. 1936

– *Satires and Epistles*, edited by J.B. Greenough. Boston: Ginn & Co. 1915

Hughes, Gethin '*Versos bimembres* and Parallelism in the Poetry of Francisco de la Torre' *HR* 43 (1975): 381–92

Hurtado de Mendoza, Diego *Obras poéticas*, edited by William I. Knapp. Madrid: Miguel Ginesta 1877

Iventosch, Herman 'Cervantes and Courtly Love: The Grisostomo-Marcela Episode of *Don Quixote*' *PMLA* 89 (1974): 64–76

Juan de la Cruz, San *Obras completas*, edited by P. José Vicente de la Eucaristía. Madrid: Editorial de Espiritualidad 1957

Kayser, Wolfgang *Interpretación y análisis de la obra literaria* 4th ed. rev. Madrid: Gredos 1961

Keniston, Hayward *The Syntax of Castilian Prose: The Sixteenth Century* Chicago: University of Chicago Press 1937

Komanecky, Peter M. 'Quevedo's Notes on Herrera: the Involvement of Francisco de la Torre in the Controversy over Góngora' *BHS* 52 (1975): 123–33

Kossoff, David *Vocabulario de la obra poética de Herrera* Madrid: Real Academia Española 1966

Kristeller, P.O. *Renaissance Thought* New York: Harper & Row 1961

Lapesa, Rafael *Historia de la lengua española* 5th ed. Madrid: Esciler 1962

– 'La poesía de Gutierre de Cetina' *Hommage à Ernest Martinenche* Paris: Editions d'Artrey, n.d., 248–61

– *La trayectoria poética de Garcilaso* 2d ed. Madrid: Revista de Occidente 1968

– 'Más sobre atribuciones a Gutierre de Cetina' *Homenaje a Emilio Alarcos* Valladolid: Universidad de Valladolid 1 (1965), 275–80

– 'Poesía de cancionero y poesía italianizante' *Strenae* Salamanca: Universidad de Salamanca 1962, 259–79

Laynez, Pedro *Obras*, edited by Joaquín de Entrambasaguas. 2 vols. Madrid: CSIC 1951

Lázaro Carreter, Fernando *Estilo barroco y personalidad creadora* Salamanca: Anaya 1966

León, Fray Luis de *La poesía*, edited by O. Macrí. Salamanca: Anaya 1970

– *The Original Poems*, edited by Edward Sarmiento. Manchester: Manchester University Press 1953

Lessig, Doris *Ursprung und Entwicklung der Spanischen Ekloge bis 1650* Geneva: Librairie Droz 1962

Levin, Harry *The Myth of the Golden Age in the Renaissance* Bloomington: Indiana University Press 1969

Lewis, C.S. *The Allegory of Love* Oxford: Oxford University Press 1951

Lillo Rodelgo, J. *El sentimiento de la naturaleza en la pintura y en la literatura española* Toledo: Serrano 1929

Lincoln, Eleanor, ed. *Pastoral and Romance: Modern Essays in Criticism* Englewood Cliffs: Prentice-Hall 1969

Lomas Cantoral, Jerónimo de *Obras* Madrid: Pierres Casin 1578

López Bueno, Begoña *Gutierre de Cetina. Poeta del renacimiento español* Seville: Diputación Provincial 1978

López Estrada, Francisco *La 'Galatea' de Cervantes* La Laguna de Tenerife: Universidad de Tenerife 1948
- 'Sobre la fortuna y el hado en la literatura pastoril' *BRAE* 26 (1947): 431–42
MacAndrew, R.M. *Naturalism in Spanish Poetry from the Origins to 1900* Aberdeen: Milne & Hutchinson 1931
Malkiel, María Rosa Lida de *Juan de Mena* Mexico: Nueva Revista de Filología Hispánica 1950
- 'Transmisión y recreación de temas grecolatinas en la poesía lírica española' *RFH* 1 (1940): 21–63
Manrique, Jorge *Obra completa*, edited by Augusto Cortina. 8th ed. Buenos Aires: Espasa-Calpe 1966
Marinelli, P.V. *Pastoral* London: Methuen 1971
Medina, José Toribio *Vida de Ercilla* Mexico: Biblioteca Americana 1948
Mele, Eugenio 'Sobre canciones y sonetos italianos y españoles' *Revista castellana* 5 (1919): 209–22
Mele, Eugenio, and González Palencia, Angel 'Notas sobre Francisco de Figueroa' *RFE* 25 (1941): 333–82
Meléndez Valdés, J. *Poesías*, edited by P. Salinas. Madrid: Espasa-Calpe 1925
Mena, Juan de *El laberinto de fortuna*, edited by José Manuel Blecua. Madrid: Espasa-Calpe 1960
Menéndez Pelayo, Marcelino *Historia de las ideas estéticas en España* 3d ed. vol. 2. Madrid: CSIC 1962
- *Horacio en España* 2 vols. Madrid: Dubrull 1885
Menéndez Pidal, Ramón *Manual de gramática histórica española* 11th ed. Madrid: Espasa-Calpe 1962
- 'Observaciones sobre las poesías de Francisco de Figueroa' *BRAE* 2 (1915): 333–83; 458–96
Merrill, R.V., with Clements, R.J. *Platonism in French Renaissance Poetry* New York: New York University Press 1967
Montemayor, Jorge de *El Cancionero*, edited by Angel González Palencia. Madrid: Espasa-Calpe 1932
- *La Diana*, edited by Francisco López Estrada. 3d ed. Madrid: Espasa-Calpe 1962
Montero, Adalmiro 'El Bachiller Francisco de la Torre. ¿Fue el traductor de Juan Owen?' *Revista Contemporánea* 97 (1895): 346–53; 479–85
Montoliú, Manuel de *Manual de historia de la literatura española* 2 vols. 6th ed. Barcelona: Editorial Cervantes 1957
Moratín, Leandro Fernández de *Obras póstumas* Madrid: Rivadeneyra 1867
Morreale, Margherita *Castiglione y Boscán: el ideal cortesano en el renacimiento español* 2 vols. Madrid: Real Academia Española 1959

Navarro Tomás, Tomás *Métrica española* New York: Compañía General de Ediciones 1966

Nelson, J.C. *Renaissance Theory of Love* New York: Columbia University Press 1958

Orozco Díaz, Emilio *Amor, poesía y pintura en Carrillo de Sotomayor* Granada: Universidad de Granada 1967

– *Manierismo y barroco* Salamanca: Anaya 1970

– *Paisaje y sentimiento de la naturaleza en la poesía española* Madrid: Editorial Prensa 1968

– *Temas del barroco* Granada: Universidad de Granada 1947

Pabst, W. *La creación gongorina en los poemas 'Polifemo' y 'Soledades,'* translated by Nicolás Marín. Madrid: CSIC 1966

Palomo, María del Pilar *La poesía de la edad barroca* Madrid: Sociedad General Española de Librería 1975

Passavant, J.D. *Raphael D'Urbin et son père Giovani Santi,* translated by Jules Lunteschutz. Paris: Vve J. Renouard 1860

Pearsall, D.A., and Slater, E. *Landscapes and Seasons of the Medieval World* Toronto: University of Toronto Press 1973

Perella, Nicolas, J. *The Kiss, Sacred and Profane* Los Angeles: University of California Press 1969

Petrarca, Francesco *Canzioniere,* edited by Gainfranco Contini. Turin: G. Einaudi 1966

Plato *The Symposium,* translated by W. Hamilton. London: Penguin 1965

Polo, Gil *Diana enamorada,* edited by Rafael Ferreres. Madrid: Espasa-Calpe 1953

Quevedo, Francisco de *An Anthology of Quevedo's Poetry,* edited by R.M. Price. Manchester: Manchester University Press 1969

– *Obras completas: poesía original,* edited by José Manuel Blecua. Barcelona: Planeta 1963

Quintana, Manuel José, ed. *Poesías selectas castellanas* vol. I. Madrid: Fuentenebros y Compañía 1807

Rico, Francisco *El pequeño mundo del hombre* Madrid: Castalia 1970

Riquer, Martín de., ed. *La lírica de los trovadores* vol. I. Barcelona: Escuela de Filología 1948

Rivers, Elias 'On the Text of Garcilaso' *HR* 42 (1974): 43–9

– 'The Horatian Epistle and its Introduction into Spanish Literature' *HR* 22 (1954): 175–94

Rivers, Elias, ed. *Renaissance and Baroque Poetry of Spain* New York: Dell 1966

Robb, Nesca *Neoplatonism of the Italian Renaissance* 1935; reprinted New York: Octagon Books Inc. 1968

Rodríguez Marín, Francisco, ed. *Luis Barahona de Soto* Madrid: Real Academia Española 1903

Rogers, Edith 'El color en la poesía española del renacimiento y del barroco' *RFE* 47 (1964): 247–61

Sannazaro, Jacopo *Opere*, edited by Enrique Carrara. Turin: Editrice Torinese 1952

Sarmiento, Eduardo *Concordancia de las obras poéticas en castellano de Garcilaso de la Vega* Madrid: Castalia 1970

Schevill, Rudolph *Ovid and the Renaissance in Spain* Berkeley: University of California Press 1913

Segura Covarsí, Enrique *La canción petrarquista en la lírica española del siglo de oro* Madrid: CSIC 1949

Selig, K.L. 'Garcilaso in Sixteenth-Century England' *RF* 84 (1972): 368–71
- 'Two Unknown Poems by Francisco de la Torre' *Revue Belge de Philologie et l'Histoire* 36 (1958): 851–3

Sena, Jorge de *Francisco de la Torre e D. João de Almeida* Paris: Centro Cultural Português 1974

Serrano Poncela, Segundo *Formas de vida hispánica* Madrid: Gredos 1963

Seznec, Jean *The Survival of the Pagan Gods*, translated by Barbara F. Sessions. New York: Pantheon 1961

Silvestre, Gregorio *Poesías*, edited by A. Marín Ocete. Granada: Universidad de Granada 1939

Snell, Bruno 'The Discovery of a Spiritual Landscape' in *The Discovery of the Mind: The Greek Origins of European Thought*, translated by T.G. Rosenmeyer. New York: Harper & Row 1960, 281–309

Sobejano, Gonzalo *El epíteto en la lírica española* 2d ed. rev. Madrid: Gredos 1970

Stagg, G.L. 'Tmesis in the Verse of Fray Luis de León and Others: a Western Romance Mannerism' in *Linguistic and Literary Studies in Honor of Helmut A. Hatzfeld* Washington: Catholic University of America Press 1964, 385–92

Tansillo, Luigi *Il Canzoniere*, edited by Erasmo Percopo. Naples: Artigianelli 1926

Tayler, E.W. *Nature and Art in Renaissance Literature* New York: Columbia University Press 1964

Terzano, Enriqueta '[Un poeta no identificado]: Francisco de la Torre' *Nosotros* 13 (1940): 93–8

Ticknor, George *History of Spanish Literature* 3 vols. New York: Harper & Brothers 1849

Torre, Francisco de la *Poesías*, edited by Alonso Zamora Vicente. Madrid: Espasa-Calpe 1956

Valency, M. *In Praise of Love* New York: Macmillan 1961

Vega, Lope de 'El Laurel de Apolo' in *BAE* 38 (1856): 187–229
– *Obras poéticas*, edited by José Manuel Blecua, vol. 1. Barcelona: Planeta 1969
Vergilius Maro, Publius *The Aeneid*, edited by T.E. Page. 1894; reprinted
  London: Macmillan & Co. Ltd. 1955
– *The Eclogues*, translated by A.J. Boyle. Melbourne: The Hawthorn Press 1976
Vilanova, Antonio *Las fuentes del Polifemo* 2 vols. Madrid: CSIC 1957
Vossler, Karl *Introducción a la literatura española del siglo de oro* 3d ed. Mexico:
  Espasa-Calpe 1961
– *La poesía de la soledad en España* Buenos Aires: Losada 1946
Wardropper, Bruce, ed. *Spanish Poetry of the Golden Age* New York: Meredith
  Corp. 1971
Wilson, E.M., and Askins, A. 'History of a Refrain: "De la dulce mi enemiga"'
  MLN 85 (1970): 138–56
Woods, M.J. *The Poet and the Natural World in the Age of Góngora* Oxford:
  Oxford University Press 1978
Zamora Vicente, Alonso *De Garcilaso a Valle-Inclán* Buenos Aires: Editorial
  Sudamericana 1950
Zardoya, Concha 'Valores cromáticos de la poesía de Garcilaso' *CA* 110–11
  (1960): 221–37

Index

UNIVERSITY OF TORONTO ROMANCE SERIES

Lightning Source UK Ltd.
Milton Keynes UK
UKHW010014210722
406167UK00002B/451